16 REASONS WHY YOUR BUSINESS SUCKS

HOW TO BE FREAKIN' AWESOME AT EVERY LEVEL OF YOUR BUSINESS, LEADERSHIP, PROFITS, & BUILD YOUR OWN DREAM TEAM!

MARK MINARD

16 Reasons Why Your Business Sucks
How to Be Freakin' Awesome at Every Level of Your Business, Leadership, Profits, & Build Your Own Dream Team

ISBN 978-1-7347429-4-7 paperback
ISBN 978-1-7347429-1-6 eBook
ISBN 978-1-7347429-3-0 audiobook
ISBN 978-1-7347429-0-9 hardcover

Edited by:
Jennifer Harshman

Dedication

To the members of the Dream Team, who are changing lives every day for the amazing individuals with developmental disabilities we are honored to serve at Dreamshine.

CONTENTS

FOREWORD

For the past eight years, I've had the opportunity to work not only for but also alongside Mark, learning and growing in leadership on so many different levels. Before being a part of the Dream Team, I would have said no if you would have asked me if I enjoyed leadership. Ask me this same question today, and my answer is 100 percent yes—I love it. I have the privilege to have an amazing leader and mentor who continues to elevate his entire team to amazing new levels.

Mark has pushed me to be the best version of myself. In past leadership roles, I focused more on the tasks at hand than the people I served. I was often out of tune with my team, seeing them just as employees sometimes. (Sad, right?) I've learned from Mark that when you focus on the people, then you never have to worry about the task. You get dedication, commitment, and unity—and unity is power. This philosophy has transformed Mark's team into what it is today.

How do you get to this level?

I've asked myself this many times. As Mark has taught me, it's not easy, but you must shift your mindset, always think outside the box, and, most importantly never, never, never give up. You must be selfless, willing to learn, grow, and teach daily. Accept that your way is not always the right way. Learn about your team, their strengths and weaknesses, and pull them out to their fullest potential. Take accountability for your actions and mistakes. It's OK to be vulnerable—we're all human. Use a self-employed mentality, and if you can delegate this mindset to your team, nothing can stop them. Then, you'll be able to work *on* your business, not constantly *in* it. Recognize and celebrate each team member's performance and success, and know they are a vital role in making your business successful. When you show appreciation, you will get dedication. Team unity starts with bringing your team together and showing how our differences contribute to success in different ways. This will open the door to so many new levels.

I've watched Mark execute all the above while continuing to create great leaders. He pushes his team to its fullest potential while hurdling many obstacles along the way. And he'll never give up. I'm thankful for Mark pushing me all these years. He's intense, passionate, and focused on all aspects of his life and will continue to be successful in all that he does, especially leadership! This is a snapshot of what Mark has taught me in my time on his team. *Sixteen Reasons Why Your Business Sucks* is a no-nonsense guide written in Mark's signature style that's as entertaining as it is informative. It provides a whole new perspective on what it means to be a leader. Enjoy!

—Danielle Horne, Program Director, Dreamshine

INTRODUCTION

Elevating Beyond

Yeah, your business sucks. Or you're experiencing some level of suckiness, somewhere. Why else would you have picked up this book?

My entire *life* sucked at one point, which you'll read about throughout this book. At age 17, I was in jail, completely unable to recognize myself in the mugshots. That's how messed up I was. And somehow, I elevated beyond all the crap to host my own podcast. It's even landed on the top 100 list on iTunes, which still blows my mind. Check out "Elevating Beyond" for hundreds of amazing conversations I've been able to have with some of the greatest leaders from around the world, sharing their story behind this story.

As you'll learn, I started my business, Dreamshine, at the height of the recession of 2008. My office was literally in a barn as I set about to create the first-ever campus of its kind for individuals with disabilities.

During 13 years of entrepreneurship, I've seen it *all*:

- lawsuits
- contractor issues
- subcontractor issues
- hiring & firing
- dealing with conflict and drama at every possible level

- doubt, fear, panic, and anxiety
- challenges (internally and externally)
- financial ups and downs
- failures
- successes

It's been freakin' crazy, but I've also learned *tons* of lessons on handling the suck factor. I learned how to develop leadership as a skill. I've been able to do some amazing things with Dreamshine. We have the lowest turnover rate in our industry—11%, while the entire state of Ohio is at 74% or higher. And I've learned to build a rockstar team, the Dream Team. It's all been the result of continuing to take action.

I wrote this book because the so-called "experts" with no actual, successful experience make me want to gag on my protein bar.

Everyone keeps blabbering about the statistics: 30% of businesses fail within the first year, 50% within five years, and 80% within 10 years.

But guess what? I beat the statistics, and you can, too, by being willing to transform the suckiness into awesomeness. Owning a business and being an entrepreneur is played out as sexy, just flying on private jets and all this crap that the fake people show you on social media. It's getting into the grit and grime, getting dirty, and fighting from the trenches in a battle. I have the scars to prove it. We must wear those scars as badges of honor.

Leadership isn't just about making better employees. It's about creating better people. It's about empowering others on your team to become the best versions of themselves. This begins with figuring out why the heck you're doing this, anyway.

Owning a business is one of the hardest things I've ever done— harder than waking up in that jail cell, nearly dead. But it's also one of the most rewarding things I've ever done. I've been able to create an organization along with my amazing Dream Team, transforming the lives of hundreds of individuals with developmental disabilities who we are honored to serve. Growing a culture of unity and purpose has made an enormous impact on family lives and relationships, making better husbands, wives, and parents who can grow and chase their dreams. We now have unstoppable momentum.

Throughout this book, I'll be providing worksheets that *work*, along with some of my favorite truth bombs to challenge your mindset to grow and equip you to take massive action. To be freakin' awesome at every level of your business. So here we go. (And by the way, I'll be using the word *freakin'* a *lot* in this book. Feel free to hit me up with the exact amount.)

Truth Bomb

Leadership means that when all hell breaks loose, you must climb out through the fire, inspiring your team along the way while silently enduring the pain of the flames.

CHAPTER

Your "WHY" Sucks

I f you only got into this for the money, if you're hoping for a magical wish to come true, or if you don't have a strong enough "why," you will be one of those 30, 50, or 80 percent who will fail. Not *if* but *when* the storms hit, if you don't have a strong enough foundational "why," your wishes will wash away. This is what it means to be freakin' wishy washy. You'll give up with no persistence or commitment.

So how do you move forward?

The "why" and the "how" are different. The "why" connects to your purpose—something bigger than you. It's OK not to know the how. If you have a "why" and continue to take action, you will figure out the "how" along the way.

"If you do the work you love," writes Dan Miller, "you'll never have to work another day again." Miller, the best-selling author of *48 Days to the Work You Love*, wrote the forward to my book, *The Story of You: Transforming Adversity into Adventure.* I like to add a twist to his often-quoted phrase: "When you do the work you love, you'll actually work harder than you've ever worked in your life." But your "why" will power you through the hard work.

So why did you really start your business? Or, if your starting one, why do you want to start a business? Tired of working for someone else? Dreaming of quick riches?

What about the true meaning or purpose behind your business and your vision? At the end of this chapter, I'll give you a self-assessment based on your "why" to help you determine if you'll succeed.

How I Found My Way Out of a Jail Cell and Into My "Why"

My company, Dreamshine, dates back to when I was 17 and jolted awake in a jail cell with no clue how I got there. All I could feel was the cold concrete. The warden—a grisly man with a beard—opened the cell door, and I saw a police officer. *I'm in jail*, I thought, numbed with shock. He explained I'd been arrested for drunk driving and took mugshots. I couldn't recognize myself. *Who's that guy with the smashed face?* Then the pain hit; I soon learned my left eye socket had been fractured and my jaw broken. My blood alcohol had been so high, the officer said, he read the report and just assumed I was dead.

I was terrified. I could have died?! As I was going through the process with the judge, he flipped me out of my victim mindset, making me think: "Forget about you. Thank God you didn't kill someone else." I'd been living in a trailer with two other dudes, doing all kinds of stupid things, choosing to be a freakin' loser.

Successful people were just born that way, I figured. What a bunch of BS, I realized—as I began reading transformational books at age 18. Gradually, I turned my life around, cutting the toxic people out of my life, changing my mindset—even going to college and getting involved in working out.

I'd always had a strong work ethic. I'd even worked my first job at Taco Bell at age 15. But I had a weak mindset. The moment I realized I was the problem—and also the solution—my mindset changed.

This, by the way, applies to you reading this right now at whatever level of suckiness you're facing with your business. Summers I spent working for my older brother's tile company, doing hard labor. But I didn't want to be looked at as, "Oh, that's the owner's little brother; he can just coast along." That fueled me to want to work 10 times harder than everyone else.

This was also one of the first times I saw my brother as someone who'd created a business, truly as an entrepreneur. It made me think, *Wow! Maybe if I do everything just right, I could own my own company one day.* I didn't know what I wanted to do, but I ended up with a degree, just a BS in psychology. Through a series of events, I landed several different jobs that led me to the field of working with individuals with special needs. I immediately fell in love with it.

The only option for young people with developmental disabilities after high school were these horrible, institutionalized "workshops," which looked like giant factories, with disgusting fluorescent lights. Many of them needed full physical assistance with eating, clothing themselves, toileting, and taking medicine. Some had severe behavioral issues and were suffering seizures and so much more. I saw about 16 of them sitting around a table with nothing to do all day but sometimes put machine parts together. Or they were given a piece of paper with crayons and told to color. They were treated terribly and not given any attention.

It pissed me off to see that these were the only options. I'd always been for the underdog. Something had to be done about it. And I knew there could be something better out there for them.

That's when I realized I could step up and do something about it.

What if I created my own agency? For a full year, I researched every state and Medicaid rule and learned everything it would take to become certified. I met with other independent operators, including one in another region of Ohio who had a beautiful program on a horse farm. He shared some of his challenges with the county-owned funding in opening his own agency. "You'll be one of the first on that side of Ohio to do it," he said. "Be prepared for battle." He told me some of his war stories, which included even taking the county and the state to court, fighting them to open his company and serve his individuals. It took many months, but he won and had the battle scars to show me and prepare me.

I was able to see the amazing possibilities out there, which pushed me further toward my vision of creating a beautiful resort-like atmosphere with options based on each amazing individual's needs. It was hard work, but it was also my "why." And when the times got really tough and I felt like throwing in the towel and thought I couldn't do it anymore, I'd think of people like Brian Brooks, a young man with autism. I'd met him along with his mom, Tammy, through working in special education where I used to provide care for Brian on the weekends. As I got to know Tammy more, she shared with me that she had quit her career to make a way that she would be able to work from home so she could take care of her son, Brian, who was miserable at the institutionalized workshops screaming and digging into his skin. She dreamed of a better place, where he could be active and have so many more different options to have friends, socialize, and be happy. To have freedom.

I was 26 years old when I started Dreamshine, newly married with three young kids. My wife was working the overnight shift, and I was getting no sleep. To top it off, I got a call out of the blue from a lady who worked high up in the State of Ohio telling me that she was trying to "do me a favor," and I should not open up Dreamshine. She said that she and her colleagues have been doing these programs for about 20 years and that they had no need for an agency like mine to open and get in their way. Basically, she was threatening me not to open Dreamshine. I told her, "Thank you so much for your wonderful 'advice.' Don't ever call me again."

These are perfect examples of why you need to have a "why." When those storms hit, I'd remember Brian and tell myself, "You don't get to give up."

Today, Brian enjoys time with his friends at Dreamshine. He's been attending for 13 years, relaxing on our beautiful 2.5 acre campus. He makes soy wax candles for our online Dreamshine store. And he enjoys outings with the Dream Team, including a recent Harlem Wizards game, along fishing in our Dreamshine pond—fully stocked with fish—ballroom dancing, and so much more.

When you find something that is bigger than you, it keeps you going and pushes you through those tough times—such as when I fought the county superintendent tooth and nail to enroll our first client.

The challenges continued: convincing families who'd not only been stripped of all support, but also lied to by county officials who said only they had the funding for their programs, and insurance didn't cover our private program. A flat-out lie. And that's where I had to keep spending thousands of hours learning every Medicaid and Medicare rule. My mentor hadn't said it would be easy, and I'm telling you, it's not easy. It's not going to be. But you need to keep becoming the best at whatever it is you're doing.

I pretty much became a self-taught lawyer, and I was able to keep battling with the State to show them, by their own rules and laws, that we had not only the same certifications, but also the correct insurance and funding. At one point, I said I'd need to report the whole State of Ohio to the federal level that they were committing Medicaid fraud and neglecting individuals with developmental disabilities by preventing them from coming to Dreamshine. And I kept going through these battles and showing them the exact rules and laws. This went on for months, and we continue to fight with the State. It was exhausting.

But because I had a strong "why," Dreamshine now serves 55 people with disabilities and more than 20 team members—the Dream Team—working alongside them. As I tell them, they are changing lives every day. Our program is the best there is, and we're honored to have a wait list for individuals as we continue to grow and expand.

My "why" didn't suck. My "why" took me from a barn in 2007 to the Dreamshine campus, and beyond. It helped me start a podcast, "Elevating Beyond" that now has more than 4 million downloads in more than 55 countries, and counting.

I've discovered how there are different levels of "why" for different seasons in our lives. From working with Brian and creating Dreamshine to tapping into leadership and empowering other team members in an amazing culture, my "why" reaches new levels all the time.

And now, with this book, my "why" is even stronger. As I've been hosting our own events on leadership and reasons why your business sucks at our own Dreamshine campus and speaking at other companies, my "why" is even stronger. Yours will be, too.

Discovering *Your* "Why"

As I was earning my B.S. in Psychology, they had us students study and learn all different types of personality tests, which to be honest, most of them were a freakin' joke. I am never a fan of trying to put limits and labels on people. However, personally, one test that we've continually used over the years which is so spot on time and time again, is the DISC test. I've been trained on the DISC test, and teach it, which helps you understand yourself, your strengths, and your weaknesses, and what to work on. How you communicate with others is also a big part of the DISC test and can help you discover your "why.".

We have all different personalities at Dreamshine, and the DISC test connects with our purpose—the purpose of knowing we're changing lives for individuals with disabilities in our strong, serving leadership team. So much of this test is connected to understanding where your strengths and weaknesses lie to help position yourself to be in the best spot to serve your purpose. The DISC test goes way more in-depth than what I'm sharing here. That would take a whole other book, but it's hugely important which is why we teach and do training on it. (For more information on the DISC test, go to markminard.net)

For a quick summary of the DISC test, it is compiled of four main categories:

D: Decisive
I: Interactive
S: Stabilizing
C: Cautious

Out of these, I'm a super high D: Decisive. Once I discovered my "why," there was no turning back. Here's a quick summary of each:

Decisive: Decisive tends to be in positions of leadership and has the mentality—ready, fire, aim—quick to take action.

Interactive: Interactive is usually very outgoing and is the life of the party. They have a lot of great energy.

Stabilizing: Stabilizing has a great loyalty characteristic and is known to play a great role in bringing peace to the group.

"When I first discovered this thing called the WHY, it came at a time in my life when I needed it. IT wasn't an academic or intellectual pursuit; I had fallen out of love with my work and found myself in a very dark place. There was nothing wrong with the quality of my work or my job, per se; it was the enjoyment I had for the work that I'd lost. By all superficial measurements, I should have been happy. I made a good living. I worked with great clients. The problem was, I didn't feel it. I was no longer fulfilled by my work, and I needed to find a way to rekindle my passion. The discovery of WHY completely changed my view of the world and discovering my own WHY restored my passion to a degree multiple times greater than at any other time in my life."—Simon Sinek, *Start With WHY*

Cautious: Cautious is very organized and tends to be extremely naturally skilled in organization. It's on the flip side of the D and has the mentality of ready, aim, aim, aim, fire.

The DISC enhances self-awareness and spotlights your strengths. It shows you areas that you need to work on to be better equipped as you continue to develop and keep moving to the next level on discovering your "why."

Truth Bomb

When you do the work you love, you'll actually work harder than you've ever worked in your life. And it will be more rewarding than you could have ever possibly imagined.

The Why Challenge

Answer the questions below to identify if your current "why" is strong enough.

1. Why did you start your company?

_____
_____
_____
_____

2. What makes you passionate about your industry or business?

_____
_____
_____
_____

3. Who will benefit if everything goes exactly as you want it to with your business?

_____
_____
_____
_____

4. What are you risking if everything goes wrong?

_____
_____
_____
_____

5. If you were to give up on this dream in your heart right now, who would be affected?

_____
_____
_____
_____

CHAPTER

You Suck at Delegating: How to Delegate Your Mindset

"Unbelievable!" I muttered to myself. "Why can't you just do the job the right way—this is why I hired you!"

It was during the first few years at Dreamshine, and I was frustrated that my program manager couldn't read my mind. He should just know from the job description, right? I was *awesome* at reading his mind, I thought. We were wasting time, and I was getting really irritated.

"Just let me handle this," I said, grabbing a stack of papers. My line of thinking was: If you want something done right, you have to do it yourself.

Then it dawned on me, what if he *can't* read my mind? What if I can't read his mind? What if I actually got the courage to sit down with him and lay all the cards on the table? We might come up with a system to figure out and solve the problem.

Sound familiar? Good delegation skills are a must for a strong leader. But before delegating tasks, you need to delegate your mindset, which I'll teach you in this chapter.

I was the problem—and also the solution.

The story above illustrates how my assumptions about delegation were part of a fixed mindset I'd learned from the business world. Immediately hire someone to do everything you don't want to do, or that you think you shouldn't be doing.

Because of this mindset, I went through several team members I thought just weren't good enough. I was so busy delegating the "how" instead of the "why." I expected them to magically be able to read my mind. Since they had experience being a manager somewhere else, they should immediately know how to become a manager at Dreamshine, right?

Nope. I freakin' sucked at delegating. What I learned over time is how delegating effectively means *delegating your mindset* instead of general tasks to an employee or your team members. You must create an atmosphere where you're not just worshiping procedures and saying, "We do this because it's policy."

You need to explain the why behind a procedure so they can understand how it affects the organization, the individuals, and the other staff members at a broader level.

We've been able to do several events over the years through my speaking. I've connected with so many other incredible business owners and leaders through my podcast, "Elevating Beyond." They have actual experience in the trenches after decades of running and building their businesses successfully.

At one of our recent events, Minutes with Millionaires, my good man, Bill Cortright, was there. Bill has owned several very successful companies for decades. When Bill decided to bring his son, Super Millennial, on board, he wanted to teach him the importance of what it really took, and not show him favoritism and just give it to him easy.

Bill even made him apply for a second job working at Best Buy. That's how important work ethic and grind are to Bill.

During our Q&A session, Bill gave an example of a good work culture. During Super Millennial's interview process at Best Buy, they asked him what he would do if he faced a problem he couldn't fix. "I'd think of ways to solve the problem and try to be resourceful," said Super Millennial. "Then if I couldn't problem-solve on my own, I'd reach out to a manager to help."

The response? "*No!* That's the wrong answer. You should *immediately* go to your manager."

I was blown away. It's the *opposite* of what we do at Dreamshine. It's the opposite of what every great culture does. This fails to create leaders— it creates robots who malfunction when something goes out of order. It destroys unity among team members. This is what makes businesses start to suck. They have mediocre cultures, and they become stagnant.

Instead, let's *teach* them to have a problem-solving mindset, which actually puts out more fires and builds momentum for the organization as a whole.

How To Delegate Mindset

It all starts with monkeys. That's right, freakin' monkeys.

In the *One Minute Manager*, Ken Blanchard and Spencer Johnson asks us to imagine we're surrounded by a bunch of monkeys as we go through our work days. Your team members come by your desk with all kinds of monkeys on their shoulders. Then you're dealing with your monkeys while their monkeys jump onto your desk. What a mess. Teach them to take their monkeys with them when they leave and, better yet, they should grab some of your monkeys to take with them, too.

If they come in and say, "Mark, you have a problem," the verbiage must change.

"We are a team; *we* have a problem. Don't give me your freakin' monkey." Already, you're delegating your mindset by retraining *their* mindset: this is not a you/me problem. This is a team problem.

12

The next time your team members come by with their problems, follow these five steps:

1. Ask them to see the monkeys jumping off their shoulders onto your desk. This is when you ask just what the problem is.
2. Walk them through how to take the monkeys back with them—solve the problem—and explain the "why" behind your reasoning. You're delegating your mindset.
3. When they return with the monkeys, still trying to fix an issue, ask them for the three best solutions.
4. Ask them to choose the top solution and explain their thinking, allowing them plenty of time to really think about it on their own, taking the monkeys with them.
5. If they return with what you think is the wrong solution, that's OK. Praise them for taking action. Coach them, and explain why. Ultimately, they'll see your mindset and will make decisions based on your company's values.

Before you know it, you'll have conversations with all of your team members where they are telling you about a problem that they've already fixed. Why? Because you took the time to delegate your mindset.

A game of horseshoes and a teachable moment.

After I've delegated my mindset to team members, I use three words to remind me how to delegate tasks: trust, time, and competency.

Trust: Be honest with yourself: Do you trust them with the task at hand? The best way for them to gain trust is for you to see that they are continually competent in completing the different tasks. As you continue to teach them and see team members growing in competency and trust, you need to not micromanage and give them more freedom to do an amazing job. But it's always important that you still keep your thumb on the pulse, and as I've heard before, check in from time to time to have a system where you "inspect what you expect."

Time: It takes longer than you think for someone to really grasp a task, and it takes even more time up front to invest in the team member and gradually allow them to handle it on their own. Yes, it takes more time to invest upfront, but will save you way more time in the long run as you continue to delegate your mindset.

Competency: Can they complete the task properly? Do they understand the ins and outs? Are they familiar with any necessary systems? Make sure you or other leaders who've delegating their mindset have witnessed them being competent and successful. When they haven't been, that's a coachable moment to make sure they're willing to grow. This is a perfect example of what I mean by "inspect what you expect."

When I started Dreamshine, I did *everything*, and one of my favorites was giving tours for potential new clients. I thought I would do it forever. But as Dreamshine grew bigger, I knew I had to delegate the task—and my

When Nate was a new employee at Dreamshine, he was responsible for setting up a game of horseshoes, which included measuring the distance between the targets. When Nate came to me and said, "You have a problem," I immediately corrected him: "No, Nate, we have a problem." It turned out he'd forgotten to buy a tape measure—and was convinced we'd have to cancel the event. Nate would be a great example of someone who fits in the high C of the DISC test. I explained to Nate the "why": the measurement didn't have to be 100% precise. I let Nate know the bigger picture of how we had horseshoes on our schedule and that our clients with developmental disabilities were already very excited to do it on this day's programming. In this instance, it's always better to do something versus nothing. I quickly showed him how he could improvise and use his foot which was about a size 12 to walk out 12 steps since we didn't have a tape measure available. And the games went on, and our individuals had an amazing time playing horseshoes. This teachable moment allowed me to help Nate solve the problem because I delegated my mindset, explained to him the "why," and also of course, followed up to make sure that he did get the tape measure to set it up the right way in the future. In this instance, it's better to do something versus nothing as perfect conditions don't always exist.

A few years later, Nate had been organizing an outing for our clients when he learned a member of our staff was in the hospital. Nate decided to take the group to the hospital instead, buying her flowers on the company card. "Oh, my gosh!" he reported back to me. "You should have seen her smile. Her mom was there. She was so happy."

My response: "That is freakin' awesome." He knew our values and my mindset and that it was OK to spend the money unauthorized. And he'd made her day.

mindset. I started training a team member who went on the tours alongside me, able to hear the important talking points and most common questions. After shadowing me, I got to shadow her. It was one of those competency times. If she'd missed the mark or didn't thoroughly explain something, I was able to help her later, behind the scenes. Pretty soon, she was giving the tours on her own. It's been four years now since I've given a tour of Dreamshine, but this allows me to work more *on* the business and not *in* the business. So I'm able to use my energy and strengths to continue to elevate and grow, taking Dreamshine to new levels by delegating my mindset to my amazing team members.

And guess what? Your team members will learn to do things better than you. They'll be independent, able to take your business to another level.

Truth Bombs

- Always delegate the why and the how. Clearly explain the task at hand, and how all the dots connect for a 360-degree vision.
- Clearly explain the tasks to team members. Don't make assumptions.
- You will never grow until you learn to *let go*. You can't do everything, or else you're always working *in* your business, unable to invest your energy into working *on* your business and leadership. Get in the habit of delegating your mindset to your team members.

CHAPTER

You Suck At Conflict

One of the most important ways to make your business not suck begins with hiring a world-class team. Let's take a brief moment to think about conflict. I've had my company for 13 years, and have been working on my show and working with other business owners, speaking, even doing consulting and coaching—from small business owners to CEOs of Fortune 500 companies. And in all honesty, one of the biggest areas they struggle with is conflict.

But the key here is that conflict can be healthy, and healthy organizations win by handling it incredibly.

Here's an example of unhealthy conflict. A woman I now think of as Ms. Passive-Aggressive applied for a job at Dreamshine, and during the third interview, shared a story about a conflict at her previous workplace. She was open and honest about being passive-aggressive, but we could tell she was still angry about it. Clearly, Ms. Passive-Aggressive hadn't learned how to handle conflict healthily.

My Three Basic Rules for Healthy Conflict

I use three basic rules to maintain healthy conflict at Dreamshine and in my personal life.

1. Don't call someone out in front of the entire team.
2. Pick up the phone instead of texting.
3. Don't leave conflict unresolved.

In my early years at Dreamshine, I broke the first rule when I called out in front of the team an employee I now remember as Mr. Negative Face. Actually, I blew up in a way that I shouldn't have. Even though he was doing wrong, one of our core values is to treat others as you would want others to treat you. The team was uncomfortable, and I looked like a jerk because guess what? I was being a freakin' jerk. I made it a point to apologize to him in front of the entire team so everyone could see I was taking accountability. Humility comes before honor. Today, I teach all my team members if conflict happens, pull the other person off to the side for a quick, standup, five-minute meeting. These are the courageous conversations where you have healthy conflict, and you leave more unified, with a weight off your shoulders. (This also relates to our no-gossip policy, which I'll discuss later.) If the conflict is still left unresolved, it's your responsibility as the leader to step in and address the conflict immediately in a healthy way. Our rule is we all leave understanding and respecting each other, and if you still have a bad attitude then you need to leave, literally, and find a job elsewhere.

And the second rule is simple. Some of us rely way too much on technology. Don't get me wrong; I text like crazy, and I love it. I think it's a great way to healthily communicate. But when it comes to conflict, you need to stop texting. Let me give you a recent example of when my 17-year-old son was driving me crazy. I was recently in a one-on-one meeting and got text after text in a row: "Dad. Dad. Come on. I need you to call me!!" Like there was some kind of fire going on.

My phone is on silent mode in meetings, but my son's texts kept flashing so much, I got concerned it was a serious emergency. I said, "I'm so sorry, it's my son, I need to quickly check what's going on." When I looked at my son's texts, I noticed they were all about my having to order pizza for him and his friends. (which was totally unannounced—apparently he invited half the football team over and "urgently" needed me to order them pizza). I texted him back that I was in a meeting and and would be happy to order a pizza for them. And he wrote back, "Fine!"

I was thinking, *Man, that little punk, so rude with that attitude.* By the time the meeting ended my heart was pounding out of my chest with anger. *"Fine!" Unbelievable.* I picked up the phone to call him and when we talked, he explained that he meant "fine" as in "cool, no problem." See the miscommunications that can happen with texts and emails?

The moment I have any conflict with a team member, contractor, or subcontractor, I pick up the phone. It's typically a game-changer, and we crush that conflict in its tracks.

Follow the 24-Hour Rule

When you're emotional, you're not rational. Think of when you've gotten a wonderful email late at night from someone who got you really angry, just flat-out pissed off.

In the moment, if you reply with what you're thinking, watch out. Follow the 24-hour rule. I'm not going to lie. I've even written up a draft email with a lot of four-letter words in it. And that was therapeutic for me. I didn't send it. I saved the draft, and got a good night's sleep. The next day, when I responded, 24 hours later, I wasn't just reacting off my emotions.

Unresolved conflict causes negativity

Here's another example from my early years at Dreamshine, when I had a team member that we now refer to as Mr. Negative Face. He was great at his job, but he would get frustrated and wasn't good at controlling his emotions. He'd lash out at times with other team members. The atmosphere was becoming toxic. And by the way, Mr. Negative Face is one of those people who are freakin' "energy vampires."

This went on for three to four weeks. I'd meet with him and say: "You're great with individuals, but they like you being toxic, and the way you're allowing your anger to lash out other team members, that needs to stop." But then it would continue, and it would be like a broken record. And what I learned was that by allowing this conflict to go on unresolved, I was being a coward. I didn't want to face this conflict in a healthy way.

This started to destroy the unity of our team because the conflict kept going on unresolved. Mr. Negative Face was draining the energy out of our organization. Later on, I even found out that some of our rockstar team members quit because of this. I eventually fired him—and we'll talk about that in another chapter—learning the hard way to never, ever, ever to allow conflict to go unresolved.

Truth Bombs

- Stop avoiding conflict. Healthy organizations have healthy conflicts.
- *Never* try to solve conflicts in an email or text message. A phone call or in-person meeting is the best way.
- Running away from conflict makes it worse for everyone involved. The longer you wait the worse it elevates.

Practice solving conflicts in a healthy way to make it a habit.

CHAPTER

You Suck At Hiring

I sucked at hiring once, too. As I began to develop Dreamshine, I had no clear strategy. I used to basically say, "OK, you have a heartbeat, you have some skills—you're hired." I brought people on board without fully thinking through what makes someone an incredible cultural and skill-set fit for the company. And then you waste tons of time and money training and then firing them.

So, I've learned that hiring just as much an art as it is a science. If you're planning to have your business stick around for the future, you'll have to master the art of *your* hiring process.

My four-step strategy for hiring looks like this:

1. Rock-star job descriptions
2. Finding rock stars: launching the hunt
3. Screening applications
4. Interviewing
   Phone interview
   In-person interview and references

Time on the floor
Lunch or dinner interview
Onboarding

I'll discuss each of these in detail before getting into the importance of tools, training, and the employee handbook. I know you're thinking, *Mark, this is crazy! You have so many steps.* I promise you these are game changers. You can do this. It will change your entire company.

> Hire slow, fire fast.

Even before you begin on the first step, start the hiring process by being *aware*. Aware that you have a gap that needs to be filled. Aware that you need more humanpower. Aware of what the position is, what it entails, and what type of person is needed to execute the required tasks. Ask yourself each day—whom do I need to bring aboard who will be best positioned to advance our mission?

Rock Star Job Descriptions

There's no freakin' way you're going to build a rock-star company with generic job descriptions from some online site. Instead, it's up to you and your trusted team members to write one for exactly the person you want to hire, starting with specific expectations, company culture, and your core values. A math-genius CPA who may have super-awesome skills might be reading your job description—and pausing over one of the core values. For example, they may

> "The strength of the team lies within the individual. And the strength of the individual lies within the team."—Phil Jackson

see the no gossip core value, and they may disagree with it saying that they want to say whatever they want. And I may say, "Awesome, you can say whatever you want somewhere else."

At Dreamshine, we openly share our mission statement and core values:

Changing lives one beautiful mindset at a time. We are honored to serve individuals with developmental disabilities, ensuring the highest quality of independence, personal growth, and social interaction on every level. And, most importantly, have fun!

- We do not gossip (no drama or negativity—energy vampires suck)!
- Humility comes before honor (we treat everyone with dignity and respect)!
- Massive personal accountability (we do not present problems; we create solutions)!
- Courage (we do not make decisions based on fear)!
- Unity is power (we work incredibly hard to fight for our passion, our "why," and we never, never, never give up)!
- Be the best you (We challenge and encourage personal growth to become the best versions of ourselves!)
- S.O.A.R (serve others abundantly, restlessly)!

Finding Rock Stars: Launching the Hunt

Now it's time to deploy your job description—but how? These are the four best ways for me.

1. Direct referrals from current team members, colleagues, friends, or family members. Do this before posting any openings—it's **the most important strategy** for finding rock stars. At Dreamshine, employees get a $300 bonus (we call it a "bounty award") for a referral who's hired and stays through the 90-day probationary period.
2. Organic (free) social media outlets, such as Facebook page, Instagram, or Twitter.
3. Organic (free) third-party sites such as Craigslist (we've found some of our best employees here).

4. Paid third-party sites such as Indeed or LinkedIn (for more options, and the highest caliber of people)

Getting Creative

Stale job descriptions are a thing of the past. Why not spend some time filming a three-minute video explaining your company's roots, as we have on our Dreamshine careers site? And there's a reason sites like Facebook and Craigslist are called organic: they attract potential hires organically, as tags and comments help spread the word about your job description. Also, on Facebook you can target your audience, by job interest, age range, and location.

Create a catchy tagline. Ours might be: "Join a team of rock stars, and help change lives for individuals with special needs by applying here." It will instantly give them a taste of your culture.

Paid Platforms

On many sites, you'll find paid sponsorship opportunities, which are often worth it. For less than $10 per day, your post could save you $100,000 after you hire the right person, instead of wasting a year's salary on someone who was hired on a whim and turned out to be the wrong fit for your company.

Sponsorships often keep your postings populating the top of the list. During a 20-day period, we received more than 350 résumés for an administrative executive assistant position.

No matter what, an awesome job posting is critical (dreamshine. site/careers).

Screening Applications

As I'm writing this, I've pulled in one of my rock-star leaders—our program director, Danielle—as we're making some new hires. We have a pile of applications and résumés stacked in front of us. I asked

Danielle, "What are some of the red flags?" Danielle replied, "One of the biggest is when you see someone who's jumped around a lot, with just a couple of months at each job. One of the biggest is when you see someone who's jumped around a lot, with just a couple of months at each job. If there's no amazing cover letter explaining the gaps or job movement, don't waste any more time.

"Cover letters are critical: do they reference a skill set, information about your company? Do they mention your website or is it some generic, pre-written cover letter that they send out everywhere?"

To filter the candidates, we make two piles: definite nos and maybes for the next steps. (Typically, 60 percent of the applications make it into the second pile.)

Then we email the screened applicants. Our questions might include:

What did you think of our website?
Why do you think that you are good for this position?
If you were to have your own private island, what would you name it and why?

The first two tell us what fit they'd be for our culture, and the private island is just for fun. One applicant said she would name the island after her daughter born with a hole in her heart—it was an emotional, powerful story, and one which had led her to want to work with individuals with developmental disabilities. On the flip side, we've had some people respond with, "What's your website?" No seriously, I'm not kidding. Obviously, if they don't have the problem skills to look up your website this helps weed them out right away. I've also had someone write in very angrily about the private island question, "I have no idea why you have this question this has nothing to do with my job!" And really in my head, "It's to help weed out psychopaths like you."

Interviewing

Phone Interview

This is a 10–15 minute conversation, where you can review job history and start to get a feel for personality. Look out for the victim mindset, negativity in their voice, and, on the flip side, accountability.

In-Person Interview and References

By now, you've taken the first few steps, so you may be feeling a sense of urgency. But by focusing on the 80/20 rule and setting a timer for 30 or 45 minutes, you'll stay on track.

This is very important for how we do the first in-person interview: Apply the 80/20 rule—which means you let them talk 80% of the time. In the past, I'd find myself sharing story after story because of course, I'm so passionate about everything we do at Dreamshine. We'd get done, and I would be like, "You're awesome. We're awesome." Give them a fist bump, and I'd be hiring them on the spot. The problem was I didn't learn a freakin' thing about them because I was talking the whole time. This is why you need to shut up and let them do the talking for at least 80% of the time to make sure you're freakin' learning more about them.

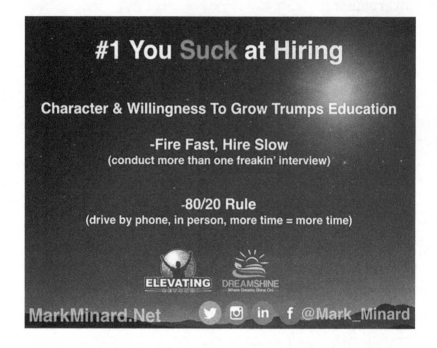

Because the interviewee is talking 80 percent of the time, it's challenging to predict exactly what your questions will be. Allow them their time, and base your questions on that. I'll typically ask more about job history or situations where they had to handle conflict.

Ask open-ended questions. Stop asking yes or no questions. This isn't a pass/fail. It's their mindset. Pay attention to cues. Are they irritated and bitter about a problematic situation? Or do they have the entitlement mindset of blaming everyone but themselves? Maybe they reveal their passive-aggressive tendencies. If they tell you how they recognized they could have done better, that shows a learning mindset.

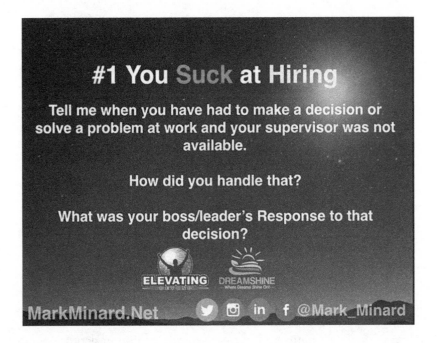

If they've made it through this interview, gather references from previous places of employment. Again, avoid asking generic questions, and insist on honesty. Instead, try, "If this person were to reapply today, would you hire them back?"

One of our employees at Dreamshine endangered clients, stole money, filed a false civil lawsuit, and then listed us for a job reference for working with foster children. No way. I let the new company know she was fired and left on bad terms. Honesty is the best policy.

Time on the Floor and the DISC test (for upper-level leadership)

The greater the position's responsibilities, the more time we spend on the interview process, which is why potential upper-level leaders take the DISC test. We'll get back to that in a moment.

The third interview is spending "time on the floor" in their potential position. We're blunt and open about the kind of work they might be doing—at Dreamshine, it could be changing an adult diaper. They meet each of our Dream Team members for a more casual conversation, and later, we'll ask our employees what they thought of the candidate.

Some of our upper-level positions take a year to fill and train because of the added responsibilities, so we add additional steps into the interview process. This includes a mandatory DISC test, which I discussed in Chapter 1. Remember, the four personality types are:

- Decisive
- Interactive
- Stabilizing
- Cautious

(Please note: this is a quick summary of the different personality styles. The DISC test is a huge tool for us because of the way it breaks down strengths and weaknesses. For a more in-depth look at the DISC test, visit markminard.net)

I go through the results with the candidate and ask some harder questions pertaining to their profile. For example, a high "C" is naturally a strength, and might indicate great organizational skills—along with passive-aggressive tendencies. So, I'll ask them about a time when they were passive-aggressive and how they handled the situation. I'm a high "D," which means I'm basically kicking doors down. But I also want to work with someone who has other strengths to help complement mine.

The whole purpose of all these steps we take through the interview process is not that any of these single things we do makes or breaks if we hire someone. What's most important is that you're gathering as much information as you can so that you're compiling it all together to be able to make the best decision possible. You gotta put on your big boy pants, or your big girl pants, and have these courageous conversations. Trust me, all these steps will be an absolute game changer as you hire that right rockstar to build up your Dream Team.

Lunch or Dinner Interview

I'm laughing as I write because I know what you're thinking: *Another interview? Are you insane?*

But it's an important last step of the hiring process, as it reveals even more about character and mindset in a much more casual atmosphere. We'll take the candidate out for a meal, inviting the spouse if they're married. Now, how are they treating the server—with respect or rudeness? Is the spouse ordering yet another beer? A friend of mine was interviewing a female candidate, and the husband had 14 drinks. He began slurring his speech and berating his wife. It was clearly an unhealthy marriage that would have affected her work.

The majority of the time, though, this can be a fun and informative way to seal the deal.

Onboarding

Congratulations. You've hired that rock-star candidate, but how do they really become part of your team? It comes down to building a culture of rock stars. How can you inspire them?

Every one of my team members is on WhatsApp, and every day, I say, "Good morning, Dream Team!" Then I'll share some type of motivational or inspirational quote. Just this morning, I shared one from Henry Ford: "Whether you think you can or can't, you're right."

Stay consistent. As the motivational speaker Zig Ziglar said, you can't just take one shower. You have to continually take showers. The same thing is true with motivation. You need to keep inspiring that excellence daily and continuing to build that culture. And the cool thing is, you'll build momentum. Your team members will start inspiring excellence—as long as you are creative and consistent in your approach.

Tools & Training

This may sound like a no-brainer, but make sure you have the right tools when you onboard an employee. Maybe it's a table saw; maybe it's software, or editing equipment for your podcast. And make sure the right person to train this new employee is available. You'd be surprised how many stories I hear of forgotten materials or delayed training. Both are just a waste of your company's time and money.

Employee Handbook

An employee handbook—printed or online—shares the roadmap of your company's culture and expectations. It provides clarity. You can continually make updates and adjustments along the way. But your core values remain the same.

Hiring from Within

Sometimes, it's hard to see what's right in front of your freakin' face. When we were looking for an executive assistant at Dreamshine, I didn't even think to post the job internally. Some of our employees were hurt, because they thought they might have had a shot at the position.

From then on, we made a point to internally give everyone the opportunity to apply and interview for jobs within. I learned to always announce a new job post with the team first, allowing them to apply. And if a

I've mentioned Danielle before, and she's a cool example of hiring from within at Dreamshine. A senior program director (a little dude with glasses who was obsessed with Harleys) was leaving on great terms. But Mr. Motorcycle's position was a big one to fill, requiring five years of experience in the field. Danielle lacked some of the experience, but she was willing to work hard, problem-solve, and grind. She got the job: the highest-paid team member with the most responsibilities. I've spent the past five years pouring more leadership into her than anyone else, and it's been great to see how this has elevated our business. I've delegated my mindset as a leader to the point where she is taking things over, and now she is working to develop other leaders. That is what it's all about.

Dream Team member refers us to someone who makes it through the 90-day probationary period, they get $300 in cash. It's all part of the unified culture at Dreamshine.

Truth Bombs

You must do your due diligence. Don't be afraid to ask for references as well as actually call previous employers.

- Fire fast, hire slow.
- Make sure whomever you hire shares the same core values of the company.
- Sometimes it takes a while to fill a role. Don't get discouraged; just be clear on the type of person you're looking for.
- Layer your hiring process understanding that you're doing everything you can to learn as much as possible about the candidate to be able to make the best decision possible.

5

You Suck at Life: The Truth About Work/Life Balance

F orget all the crap you've heard about the work/life balance. Because chances are, you've heard that you have to give up *everything* to be successful. And we've also seen the images of a perfectly round pie sliced up into perfect quarters, with each 25% representing your business, your health, your family, and your spiritual life). This is also a bunch of crap.

Managing the Seasons of Life

Instead of "giving everything up" or "achieving perfect balance," I talk about seasons of sacrifice and continually managing the tension of each season of life. It's a lifelong journey and one with so many amazing stretches, too.

I've been married to my beautiful wife, Iyeba, for more than 13 years. We have *five* kids. And when I first started Dreamshine in 2007, our two daughters, Neveah and Harjaah, were only a year and seven days apart. So, we had a newborn and a toddler. As I mentioned earlier in this book, my office was in a barn, and we were at the peak of the recession.

It was a blur of insanity. I was basically a one-man company, working countless hours (digging out snowbound vans, providing direct care, battling state politics, finances—you name it). When I got home after a super long day, my wife would hand me the girls and head out to work the overnight shift at her job. We were both working around the clock—literally—to make ends meet. Up half the night with the babies, I'd maybe get two to three hours of sleep. It was a season of sacrifice. We fought. We leveraged our credit cards to the max. By continuing to communicate, we eventually moved into a different season.

You, as a leader, need to share your vision with those closest to you, and explain how this will be a season of sacrifice. Eventually, by delegating and elevating parts of your work, you'll have your passion and a rich life, too.

You're going to be grinding at times. But eventually, as my good friend Kingsley Grant, an author and leadership speaker, says, you can look back over the year and see that you came pretty close to having that 25% in each of those categories: business, health, family, and spiritual. Sure, you might have had three months when you were working 100-hour weeks, but you've also learned to take time off.

Perfectionism Is a Killer

If you're reading this book, you want your company and your work life to thrive and become stronger. I get it. But when you continually choose your business over your family and other interests, everything gets weaker. Your company will suffer, your relationships will keel over, and your health will swirl down the bathtub drain.

Stop beating up and demanding absolute perfection from yourself every day. I'm hardly the first to recognize that perfectionism is a killer. Sure, you'll move toward a 25/25/25/25, but it's not going to be a perfect slice of pie every day. Kick perfectionism out of your life; instead, always be growing and developing to be the best version of yourself—for your team, your wife, your kids, and your spiritual life.

As I was writing *The Story of You*, which is my full life story, Iyeba was pregnant with our son, Gil. This would be another season of sacrifice: I'd be there to help my wife while running my company. But we had reached another level of leadership at Dreamshine, so I didn't need to spend every waking hour there. For six to eight months, I'd decided, I'd wake up at 4:30 a.m. every weekday and put in at least an hour of work. I didn't want to get up that early, but I knew it was just a season, and the book would never happen if I didn't make it happen.

Shortly after I was finishing my book, little Gil was born, and we both started losing sleep to the demands of a newborn. I'd try to catch more sleep in the mornings, and take care of my health by running late at night. It was another season of sacrifice, and it worked because Iyeba and I were in constant communication.

There's no such thing as perfect conditions or a perfect time. Great strength comes from being aware of the seasons. Different seasons require different strategies. You must continually create new systems to meet the demands of the season.

Set Your Own Schedule

I've been writing this book for more than two years while overseeing major renovations (including an incredible new waterfront lodge). It's meant working with banks for months, and working with builders and contractors. Sometimes, I veer the wrong way, but a number of tools get me back on track. It might be my wife grabbing me and saying, "Hey! You're coming home too late."

I've set alarms on my phone telling me to go home. I've added a standing lunch date with Iyeba to my schedule—no interruptions. One of my very good friends, author Bill Cortright, host of the Stress Mastery Podcast, has been an amazing mentor to me. He signs a contract with his wife every season of sacrifice that things will soon balance out for the best. Another friend, Eric Thomas, manages his life by waking up at 2:30 a.m. and going to bed at 8:30 p.m. He's been doing this for 20 years, because he figured out his energy peaks in the morning and dips as the day moves along. It's worked out amazingly well for him.

What's important here is that you continually have self-awareness. What works for one person isn't going to work for another. But if you're serious about it, you'll keep doing whatever it takes. Take systems for example. I have multiple alarms going off reminding me that it's time to go home. This is me holding myself accountable for an agreement that my wife and I made so that I wasn't constantly getting stuck up in the grind of being at Dreamshine way too late. I even have it set up where my assistant's alarm goes off. And she reminds me every Wednesday that I need to leave early to make sure I pick up my daughter for her music class.

All these things are important to me, and I have the self-awareness to drop my ego to know, "Hey, I need help. I need to set other systems to hold me accountable in these other areas that I'm dropping the ball in." My wife and I made a deal that we would start meeting for lunch every Thursday, and I purposely have it blocked out on my calendar. Every Thursday, it says, "Meeting my wife for lunch." No interruptions. Sometimes I even announce it to my entire team to help hold me accountable. I'm like: "If you see me here at this time, yell at me, because this is supposed to be my special time." Set up what works for you.

We must continually set up different systems and boundaries. I schedule *everything*, and I have reminders for everything. It keeps me focused for productivity, but I also can't stand having a schedule dictate every single moment. I make sure to intentionally block time out of my schedule where I have no meetings, and I know that I can use that time to think, strategize, and organize. As the leader or owner, you set the tone for your culture. Everyone's watching you. Which signals are you sending about priorities?

How to Really Unplug

When I took my family to Sierra Leone, West Africa, where Iyeba is from, I was confident that my team was at the level where I could unplug completely for an entire five weeks. Now, again, we go through different seasons. I would not have been able to do this within the first year or two of running Dreamshine. As CEOs, you know the saying is "Chief Everything Officer." It took some years of building up the right team and implementing the right systems to get to this level.

It might be a weekend trip with your family as you start your business, just to clear your mind. But I was able to get some years in and feel confident my Dream Team was at a level where I could unplug completely for an entire five weeks.

I arranged just one emergency line to reach me in the event of a true crisis. Don't get me wrong. I was worried about this and was even feeling a false sense of guilt. Those stupid voices come in and try to make you forget that you've already put in tens of thousands of hours. Like, *Who are you to think you can take a full five weeks off? What's your team going to think about that?* But it makes you more productive when you take that time for your mindset. You have to learn to put the systems in place to build your business over time and make the strategy. But it's possible.

I spent many days on the beautiful beaches of West Africa without cell phone service, spending time with my family, and observing nature. My brain seemed to be clear of the cobwebs. (There's a good reason why Bill Gates takes a "think week" every year, in seclusion with nothing but a big pile of books.)

When I returned, I felt I had new space in my head. I wanted to write a book and start a podcast. I hadn't realized this, but my mind had cleared out to allow new space for creativity and innovation and to clear my head from all the busy-ness.

With my mind cleared out, I started drawing stick figures with motivational messages, which landed me publicity on social media. I began to see a bigger vision of speaking, helping people, sharing my life story, and putting on leadership events. Looking into the future, I saw how it could all interconnect with Dreamshine and open up not only different revenue streams and different levels of my passion, but also job opportunities for our individuals with developmental disabilities. And by the way, the ripple effect of that led to writing this book you're reading right now, *16 Reasons Why Your Business Sucks*. The proceeds from this go to Dreamshine and the individuals we serve.

And, as it turned out, my team had truly kicked butt while I was in Sierra Leone. I was able to take five weeks off, and my team continued to work amazingly. While I was unplugging, they were elevating Dreamshine operations and service to entirely new levels. As leaders, we're not indispensable. Work will continue while you are away, without the whole place catching on fire. The great leaders are the ones who build companies and teams that can continue to grow and develop in their absence. You need to get out of your own way.

I now make it a point to truly maximize my vacation time each year. Let me be clear. I still freakin' grind with plenty of 100-hour weeks. But I've been fortunate to bring my family to some amazing places like Disney World, Bali, Fiji, and Dubai, where I soaked up the joy of having no internet access for a full two weeks. Now that was some work/life balance—not perfect, but good enough to keep me going for many more seasons.

Truth Bombs

- There is no such thing as "perfect" work/life balance. There are priorities depending on the season.
- Your family must be on board with your commitment to your company, or there will be conflict. Ongoing communication is key.
- Chase away the turkeys, and bring in the eagles and rock stars to be on your team.
- You can get more done with fewer of the *right* people.

- Put everything in your calendar. Personal and work. It's all about the 24 hours you have in each day.
- Build your Dream Team and then trust your team enough to handle things while you're gone. Give them an opportunity to prove themselves.
- Different seasons require different strategies.
- Stop staying, "I don't have time for..." you are in control of your time. Own it.

CHAPTER

You Suck at Being Insane: How to Be Innovative When Everyone Else Is Boring

"**M**ark, you're insane!" I hear it *all the time.* When I share my dreams or my business goals, I hear it: "Mark, you're freakin' crazy!" Have you heard it? Sometimes it's in admiration. And if it has a negative tone, those people will later be complimenting you for your business plan—or calling you lucky. But they should *always* be calling you crazy. Because at the corner of crazy and insane is where innovation lives.

Allow me to explain. We live in the information age, now more than ever. We can barely take a breath before hearing about the latest podcast, book, or motivational event. We hear about roadmaps to success and playbooks. And sure, I produce all of these, too. But whether it's me or another influencer, it's critical to find your own journey—solo or guided. So many people and businesses get too caught up on perfectly following and duplicating the roadmap of what someone else has already done, and they wonder why they get mediocre results.

Only changing the game and bringing it to the crazy, insane level will get amazing results.

There is always another way.

As I mentioned earlier, I had an incredible mentor in creating Dreamshine. Terrible workshops were about the only option at the time, but he owned a program based on a farm in my state of Ohio. I was in awe, and followed his wisdom—only I applied it to my own vision. That's what has made and continues to make Dreamshine *the* best program in the world. Remember, I was called crazy and insane by so many people and even threatened by very high authorities in my industry.

We've heard the story a billion times of how Netflix beat Blockbuster. You need to be continually elevating and innovating on every level of your business. What kind of crazy level are you at? No matter what books, podcasts, or playbooks (or heck, even I) tell you, there is always another way—your way.

Imagine you're going on a treasure hunt. In order to get the treasure, you have to kill a dragon on the way. Another dragon slayer who got half of the treasure five years ago gives you a map and a bow and arrows to kill the dragon by striking a soft spot on his neck. You're going back for the other half. You start following the exact directions, going into the misty, tropical jungles. Some of the turns are different, some of the landmarks have changed, and the map isn't as accurate as you thought it was. As you continue to follow these exact directions, getting deeper and deeper into the jungle, you run into a roaring river. What the heck? This isn't on your map. Suddenly, you're filled with fear and doubt—and you're running low on food and water.

What do you do? Do you quit the hunt, turn around, and go back? Let's say you keep going. You reach the cave on the map, and sure enough, a dragon seems to be guarding something inside. Great.

But wait a second—this dragon has no soft spot on his neck. It's coated with thick scales and armor. The bow and arrows would just bounce off. But you're not turning around now.

We don't give up. We keep going. We keep finding another way. No matter how crazy they call us. You notice a giant boulder above the mouth of the cave. You figure out a way to wedge a nearby tree branch to pry the boulder up and off the edge. You kill a rabbit with the bow and arrow, and you drop it at the mouth of the cave, where the dragon emerges to gobble it up. BAM! The boulder lands directly on top of the dragon's head, crushing it. You enter the cave and see mountains of gold coins. Rubies larger than your fist. The hoard is bigger than you could have imagined. You have discovered your treasure. You followed your instinct and your smarts—you found another way. And that is how we get all of life's richness.

Dr. Dre beats the dragon, too.

As the leader, you must continually embrace the mindset of this second dragon slayer. You'll feel the doubt and uncertainty and learn to keep doing it anyway. You'll change the game, opening up a new world of opportunities for yourself, your team, your company, and your community. Will it be easy? Hell no. Will it be hard? Hell yes. Will it be worth it? *Absolutely.*

Remember, this is bigger than you. The world is counting on you for your services and products. Your team is counting on you. You don't get to give up. The next time you're getting ready to launch a product or create something, ask yourself, "What am I doing that is different and better than everything else that's ever been done in my industry?" Then freakin' *go for it!*

Just look at NWA And Dr. Dre, whose story you should check out in the HBO documentary series, *The Defiant Ones* (definitely worth looking into, if you haven't already). It's a game changer.

In the 1980s, NWA was making music unlike *anyone* else in the music industry. Dr. Dre made rap a mainstream success. Trust me, you need to watch this entire documentary. Dr. Dre had so many dragons to slay along the way to obtain his success, but he did it. And he didn't stop there. Years later, he teamed up with the legendary record producer Jimmy Lovine and innovated his business to new levels, opening his own record label, and becoming a music producer. He heard a music sample by this guy Eminem. Everyone called Dr. Dre crazy; he couldn't sign this white dude! Eminem became one of the best-selling hip-hop artists in history. Dr. Dre then found another way to success, creating Beats headphones with Lovine through trial and error and a whole bunch of failures. They eventually sold Beats for $3 billion. How's that for some treasure?

Do you see the difference between changing the game on your own versus sticking with what everyone else is doing? Take some time to reflect on what you're doing differently in your industry.

Changing the Game Exercise:

How are you changing the game in your industry?

_____

_____

_____

_____

_____

_____

Have you done anything out of the ordinary in your industry?

_____

_____

_____

_____

_____

_____

If you could do one thing different from everyone else in your industry, what would it be?

_____

_____

_____

_____

_____

_____

What's stopping you from doing what you wrote above?

_____

_____

_____

_____

_____

_____

Truth Bombs

- People should always be calling you crazy—that's how you innovate.
- There is always another way. It's called your own way.
- Don't change for the game. Change the game.

CHAPTER

You Suck at Imagination: Using Imagination as Your Superpower

When we were children, we used to play every day together. We would spend so much time together. As you continued to get older, we still knew each other. We were friends. We didn't see each other as often, but we were still friends. But then, as you started to become a teenager and grow older, you completely abandoned me. You forgot about me. You gave up on me. And I'm telling you—don't give up on me.

Who am I? I'm your imagination! Even Einstein said it—there is power in imagination!

Dreamshine started with my vision of creating a place outdoors, non-institutionalized, and beautiful for individuals with developmental disabilities. At the time, nothing like it existed. All the state had were horrible institutions. I envisioned a pond, a log home, and a beautiful atmosphere. I would start making notes about it and writing things down about it.

Now, in the real world around me, none of it even existed yet. But the important thing about your imagination is it can create something better than anyone else could have fathomed.

Jogging the Brain

Vision boards of pictures, images, and words are great. Try also to create a board in your head: close your eyes, and use your imagination to bring that vision to life. When the tough times hit, go back and look at the real vision board. Close your eyes again. Eventually, the two will join together to help create your superpower.

When I jog, I don't close my eyes—that would be dangerous—but I get into my head, and I start envisioning and imagining. When Dreamshine began, I'd picture our first client with special needs. We'd throw a football, and his mom would hug me. I could feel her arms around me. The dots were connecting, and the next thing I knew, it was coming true. I kept on going, though, creating another vision board in my head.

Start daydreaming!

I've seen that happen with everything that I've ever done in my life. Do something that opens up your creativity. Your dream is different than mine. It should be. Your dream starts the moment you activate that imagination. Start acting on it.

Word Up

Think of times when, all of a sudden, you hear a new word. You've never heard it before. Say the word is *indolent*. Someone says how Joe was indolent, and you have to ask what it means (lazy). All of a sudden, you begin hearing "indolent" everywhere: on the radio, on TV. But here's the thing—it was there all along; you hear it because you focused on its meaning and now recognize it. The more you focus on something, the more you're open to it. You'll continue to notice it and pull toward it more. Like a vision board on the wall or in our heads, it tugs you out of the present moment and allows you to see something in a whole new light.

God put a vision in my heart before my book. Before my podcast. I was speaking at an auditorium filled with hundreds and thousands of people. And I didn't want the spotlight. I said: "God, no, you've got the wrong guy. I don't want that. I'm changing lives at Dreamshine. I don't want this." But it wouldn't go away.

And now here I am, speaking in auditoriums. I enjoy speaking in public, but I still get nervous, even though I've continued to do it so many times. Again, it's connected to my "why." When I'm speaking, my "why" is about sharing my message and helping other people to overcome adversity or to elevate their leadership and become better versions of themselves. That's what continues to fuel me.

What I have continued to see in my head hasn't fully manifested yet. I can't wait to see this insane vision come to life. I've always pictured a live YouTube video, but in person so that it's a full experience where there are big screens, and I'm speaking and even having a live symphony playing motivational music that perfectly flows with the different parts to enhance my delivery. It's a show and experience dropping bombs of value and changing the freakin' game of speaking.

It's the power of using your imagination and stepping into your vision. I feel myself stepping out onto the outdoor stage. I can see the lights. I can feel the warmth of the lights shining on me. I can hear the rumble of the crowd. I can feel my heart beating as I'm getting ready to step out there. I can smell the air. I can smell the field grass. It's not about the spotlight, but it's a vision that's in my heart and helping to change all of those lives and having that beautiful influence.

You go to that place. And one day, all of a sudden, you're there. People say, "You're just daydreaming," and that you need to lower your aim—go for something easier. What?! That would be lowering the bar on our own amazing imaginations. Don't do that. Don't limit yourself. Don't put other people's limits on your imagination.

Do something that you don't normally do. Start tapping into that different part of your brain.

Envision yourself, step into it, feel it, smell it, get the senses going.

A spin on taking action.

You're thinking, *Here's another person telling me how important it is to take action.* But I'm putting a spin on taking action, by forcing you out of your comfort zone. This could involve bringing on new team members, starting a new division of your company, or even taking on more clients. Be ready for the learning curve. You're going to run into things you've never experienced before. There will be new pain and new challenges.

Let me let you in on a little secret. You will *never* grow in your comfort zone. Now, if you're happy and content with where you are, then congrats. If you want more for yourself and your company, then it's time to stop sucking at taking action and do something. *Today*!

"The only way to get started is to quit talking and begin doing."— Walt Disney

Abnormal failure

This shows up in a number of ways. It can be an accident on the highway causing you to miss an important meeting with a potential new client. It can be your laptop frying the day of an important pitch presentation. It's anything that causes you to say, "Damn it, I knew I shouldn't have tried this."

Is it time to quit and go back to our comfort zones? Nope. These are actually clear signs a breakthrough is coming and you are officially leveling up. But you can't experience the breakthrough or level up unless you're taking action.

I mentioned earlier some renovations happening here at Dreamshine in an effort to serve our clients better and give them a great experience. We're working on making indoor gardens, an entirely new multisensory room, making the whole building alive with colors and lights. It's the bigger dream I always had, that Dreamshine would be like its own type of interactive Disney World, but creating options for individuals with developmental disabilities.

While that vision holds true and we're making great progress, I just ran into another issue of the contractor doubling the rates, even after working with him for months. We had all the money down for the loan, which was approved, and all of a sudden, out of the freakin' blue, boom.

But I continue to press forward. We started with another contractor, and we're making more progress, and it's turning out amazing. It's been hard, and I've had sleepless nights. You have to keep pulling the trigger and taking action.

Commit to doing at least one thing a week that literally scares you but will help you level up in your business. This is how you get in the habit of taking action. It's going to be uncomfortable, but as a business owner, you need to get used to being uncomfortable, and continue to stay out of your comfort zone until the next level becomes normal.

Level up Challenge:

Over the next 21 days, make a copy of this page and ask yourself these questions every day.

What did I do today that I've been afraid to do in the past?

_____

_____

_____

_____

_____

_____

How did it make me feel once I did it?

_____

_____

_____

_____

_____

_____

What didn't turn out the way I hoped it would? What did I learn from it?

_____

_____

_____

_____

_____

_____

CHAPTER

You Suck At Finances

Wait! Before you skip through this chapter, which you probably think is about spreadsheets, graphs, annual accounts, microeconomics, macroeconomics, and all the other crap that bores you to death, relax and take a deep breath.

Just writing those words makes me want to fall asleep. But mastering an understanding of the right way to do your finances is important. And now you get to hear it in my voice, which will be more fun, but *please* take it seriously.

When I'm speaking at events and throughout my show, different business owners reach out to me and say, "Well, Mark, you don't understand." They can't get investors, or they can't get a loan, and I keep getting more and more excuses. I always remind them I started my company in 2007, right before the recession. Join the freakin' club! I couldn't get any loans at all. It was so hard.

One of the first things you'll learn in this chapter is learning how to use credit as a strategy and a tool, not a crutch. As many of you know, Dave Ramsey tells us never to use debt. I do agree with him and have worked personally with him, but I also see how we can use debt as a tool if we're able to turn it into a strategy.

Not Tossing the Dice with Debt

When we founded Dreamshine, we had good credit, but no one would give us a loan. So, I bought two 12-passenger vans with my personal credit card. That affected my credit to the point where it was hard to get car loans and other personal items, but I did what I had to. Without providing transportation for our clients, we couldn't start.

As we grew to a point where we were running out of space in our original building, with more clients and participants, we were still in a tight spot. (This is where strategy comes in.) Credit card interest rates were close to 18%. Still, we used a credit card for nearly $30,000 to finish out the basement. Insanity! But it also allowed us to make more space to add nearly 10 more clients and participants to come to our program. It was a calculated risk. Yes, we take risks as business owners, but we're going to continue to make them calculated. It's not like closing your eyes and tossing the dice without a clue of what you're doing. You make a calculated risk and keep taking action and moving forward.

We got the basement finished. We kept up with our payments. Then, *boom*! The bank raised our interest rate from 18% to 30%. You can sit there and cry about it all day and say it's not fair. But we had made a choice, so we kept paying it off, month after month, until we cut that credit card into pieces, never to freakin' use it again. We were very intentional in making a choice to attack that and keep paying it off way above the minimum amount every month and make a strategy to keep pushing to get it paid off in full in a shorter amount of time. As Dave Ramsey says, you can get to a point where you're not using credit at all, and ultimately, I'm all for that.

Learning How to Become Your Own Bank

After the credit-card risk, I still faced financial woes. The funds wouldn't come through for payroll, and I'd be crying when I got home to Iyeba. We needed $30,000 in the account just to make payroll and other expenses coming in that week. I'd made a vow to myself to always pay my team, so it was incredibly stressful. But as a leader, that's your responsibility. You pay your own team first. Sometimes, it got so bad, I even delayed my personal mortgage payment just to make payroll, or I maxed out every one of my personal credit cards. But I'm not suggesting this is ever a strategy you continue to use in the long term. You'll end up driving yourself crazy. And it's not healthy for you or your business.

I grew sick of the cycle. I began saving money to always have payroll covered, even as I paid off other debt. My team was and always is a priority. At that time, I needed $60,000 saved up per month to cover all of our payroll and our health benefits. That was my first step, but I had a longer-term goal to have six months of all gross revenue and expenses in savings—more than $700,000—to have the money to invest in other things. We're getting closer to it each and every year, always moving that needle to keep pushing toward having that full six months in savings, as our company continues to grow.

This is what has worked for me and Dreamshine. I encourage you to continue to do what works for you.

As we are going through the final edit of this book, COVID has struck. It's mid-June 2020, and we're still battling through the pandemic. Thank God I've built up those savings during the past 13 years. Only we and one other company in our industry have managed to stay open, and Dreamshine was actually able to keep 100 percent of team members employed. Situations like this are why finances are so important.

And by the way, the unity of my team has grown to a whole new level. By having these finances set up and being able to keep team members on, we've been able to get through this season of adversity together.

Remember the story of Bill Gates going into seclusion once a year? He's also learned, like you and I, the hard way to manage money. (See *Inside Bill Gates' Brain* on Netflix.) At one point, he kept missing payroll, with insufficient savings funds. He finally made a decision to have at least one year's worth of payroll in savings before they took their business to the next level. Even billionaires have to start somewhere. As we've all heard, success leaves clues. And look what I'm showing you. This billionaire, in his own way, applied the same strategy that I'm teaching you today.

Ownership

When you own a company with investors, make sure you own at least 51% so that you are the majority shareholder and you override the decisions of others. I've heard so many horror stories of when people needed money desperately and gave away a percentage of the company to the investors. Then the investors would begin to disagree with the owner's vision and even "gang up" on the owner.

Some owners have gone public with their companies. Look at my good man Tim Fargo, who's been a guest on my show, *Elevating Beyond*, more than once and is such a solid dude. He went bankrupt with his first company, and then opened his second business. It was one of the first surveillance companies in the 1980s, and he did it with little to no credit.

Tim knew he'd have to either cut back on expenses or lose a team member, so instead of big mahogany desks, he decided they would have card tables. People would ask him, "How's that going to look?" And as Tim shared on my *Elevating Beyond* podcast, he'd answer: "We're still closing sales and have the best equipment in the country. And no one ever asks us what kind of *desks* we have. So stop worrying about stupid crap, please!"

Tim Fargo grew his company to be incredibly successful, and because he had no debt, it made the cash value of the company so high, he was able to sell it for $20 million in profit.

Truth Bombs

- Be honest with yourself regarding your money management skills. Don't wait until you're making six figures to get assistance with your company or personal finances.
- Create a savings system, and determine how much you'll put away from every client, invoice, etc. It can be as little as $10 or $100 just to get in the habit of saving.
- Open a company savings account that's completely separate from the company checking account. Avoid online access or anything that would make it easy to dip into that savings. (I even personally know some people who have a fire-proof safe that they literally put cash in.)
- Track your expenses monthly, and keep up with what you're reinvesting and what you're spending frivolously.

CHAPTER

You Suck at Being Vulnerable: The Power of Unity

No matter what you've learned in this book so far, you'll fall into the trap so many leaders, owners, and influencers have. Many times, we think we always have to be right, or that we should never admit when we're wrong. We must act like our life is perfect outside of work. Like we're superhuman. This is your ego talking. Get rid of that freakin' ego. Learn to be vulnerable—and *confident.* Always hold yourself accountable, and never be afraid to share your struggles with your team members. Let me explain this more in depth.

I've learned to over-communicate instead of under-communicate with my team. This is what *builds* unity.

If you think this makes you look weak, you're allowing your ego to control you, and this is what *prevents* unity.

The power of unity is immeasurable. It's unstoppable!

Once I **sucked** at being vulnerable, but now, most of my team members tell me that I'm the most open, honest, vulnerable leader they have ever seen. It's a lifelong process. I'm still always learning and still always growing. I've gotten so much better. I quickly admit when I'm wrong, and I always hold myself accountable when we get off track. And when my team sees this, it builds our culture to be even more unstoppable.

As I was saying before, I have a great example of how having the courage to be vulnerable and accountable as a leader trickles down and impacts the entire team.

Wins and Losses: You Start First

It takes courage to be vulnerable. It takes courage to look risky and foolish, but that's what leadership is all about. This is what led to our monthly Dream Team meetings about seven years ago. I'll never forget those first few. With transportation and such, everyone is all over the place, so we had to hold the meetings after hours and pay overtime. My sister, a co-owner at the time, wasn't on board, but I begged her to give me a shot.

I asked the team if we could start sharing our wins and our losses of the month. They could be related to Dreamshine, or it could be personal. We didn't force anyone to share. I had to start. (Like I've written, *you*, as the leader must go first. You have to risk looking stupid. You have to risk looking foolish.) I stood up and was as vulnerable as I could be, openly sharing some ongoing struggles with my son. I just asked the team for their prayers. Then other team members began talking. We've built up our trust by being vulnerable, and it's a beautiful thing.

I remember how my head program director shared her story of changing her mindset, from victim to problem-solving. Her son had just been told that he would only get half of the full-ride college scholarship promised for wrestling. When she began falling into the victim mindset, getting angry and irritated, her son interjected: "Mom! Remember what you taught me? We need to see the good in this. And if you think about it, Mom, just six months ago, we didn't even know if I was going to get into any college because I was struggling with my grades. I was able to get my grades up, and now I'm getting accepted into this incredible college—they're also going to be paying for half of my school! So this is great news, Mom! If I have to get a part-time job, I can do that!" Her family life suddenly looked a lot brighter. She began tearing up in the meeting, and most of us were, too. I'm tearing up as I write this, because of how our team vulnerability allowed such a powerful conversation to happen. This is what leadership truly is. It's what it's all about. *This* is an example of what builds true unity. It makes you unstoppable.

Our head program director went on to thank us for everything she's continued to learn at Dreamshine about leadership. She appreciated our monthly Dream Team meetings that got her to change her mindset and be able to teach this to her son. That's what hit me so hard and really made me tear up. I was so happy. I was so grateful, because this is what being a leader is all about. Leadership isn't about making better employees. It's about making better people.

And I still start first. When several of our team members began opening up about anxiety, I decided that was the moment. I not only shared my story about being in jail at age 17, but also shared my extreme anxiety and panic attacks that I've battled for most of my life. (I still battle these pretty much on a daily basis, but I've learned to overcome them.) Soon, some team members were asking for one-on-one meetings to ask for more advice on extreme anxiety. One of them has been able to cope with it so well, she's now a top leader at Dreamshine. It all starts with you, the leader, having the courage to be vulnerable.

Truth Bombs

- Encouraging others while doubting yourself doesn't make you fake. It makes you a leader.
- Being vulnerable with your team shows strength and builds unity.

- When you're not vulnerable, you can and will come off as unapproachable to your team.
- Vulnerability builds unity, which creates the powerful force of momentum, making your business and your team unstoppable.

CHAPTER 10

You Suck at Fear: Never Make Decisions Based on Fear

I talk about fear all of the time because it never goes away. Not for me, and probably not for you, either. And that's OK. But please, never make decisions based on fear.

Fear is what caused me to decide to allow Mr. Negative Face, whose story I shared earlier in this book, to stay employed too long at Dreamshine and wreak havoc on the team morale, even causing some of the super-positive team members to leave.

I've referenced the civil suit against Dreamshine a few times, too, and now, here's the whole story, which illustrates why you must never make decisions based on fear.

The Civil Suit

I'll never forget that day. It was a beautiful, sunny fall afternoon in Ohio—72 degrees, golden leaves on the trees. But it quickly clouded over in my head as I opened the mailbox to find a letter from the State of Ohio. I could hear my heart pounding as I read the words: Dreamshine was being investigated in a civil lawsuit for discrimination based on firing someone based on their gender.

Let's back it up just a bit. Remember *all* of the extra steps we talked about in the hiring process? Some of them came from this experience, after we let crazy (the bad kind) into the building.

Important note here: all of our buildings have security cameras, and this is openly posted on signs.

A woman I now call Miss Psychopath Face had tricked us into seeming like a great fit as a site manager and was actually doing pretty well in her first few months with us. One of her responsibilities was to oversee the petty cash our individuals with special needs would bring in for community outings. My sister and I started noticing how one of the books was starting to come up very short. As we confronted Miss Psychopath Face, she'd immediately come up with various reasons why the books were short. We had no other choice than to review the security videos. We discovered Miss Psychopath Face had been pilfering the petty cash.

On a Friday, when we tried to arrange a meeting with Miss Psychopath Face, she called in to say she wouldn't be coming in to work because she had an appointment come up. Our call-in policy is very strict because of the distinct needs of individuals with disabilities; it requires having a human being available there to assist them with their health and safety. It must be a true emergency or preapproved paid time off in order to miss work. (Remember when I discussed delegating mindset, and explaining the how and the why of the policy?) Miss Psychopath Face knew this as a manager. And when we asked for the doctor's information regarding her appointment, which is always standard at Dreamshine, she began cussing us out on the phone, and then, to top it off, freakin' hung up on us. We planned to meet with her on Monday (if she were to show up) and terminate her on the spot.

It was that Monday, when I just so happened to receive that wonderful letter from the State of Ohio. Here is where things get interesting. Remember, we hadn't been able to meet with her about the tapes and her stealing. We hadn't fired her, because she abruptly called in to miss the workday. We had never experienced anything like this civil suit before in our lives. Miss Psychopath Face claimed that we were discriminating against her, treating her unfairly based on the fact that she was a woman and asking her for a doctor's note. (Just to add a little fun fact here, ladies and gentlemen, at that time, my sister and I were 50/50 co-owners. It was kind of funny how Miss Psychopath Face thought she was being discriminated against as a woman. My sister has gone on to live out her other dream, running an orphanage in Ethiopia. But that's a whole other story for another day.)

We suspected Miss Psychopath Face had been planning this all along. Remember, she was caught red-handed, on camera, stealing money from our individuals with developmental disabilities. But in the State of Ohio, the law is that someone who is a minority gets representation for a civil suit, and the other party has to prove innocence.

When we told our company lawyer we needed to fire Miss Psychopath Face, he told us to be really careful. Because we'd received the letter, termination could look like retaliation, which is illegal. To sum it up, he was saying if we were to now fire her, she could twist it around. She could make it look like she wasn't fired for stealing from our clients with developmental disabilities and also for cussing us out—but that we were retaliating against her for filing this civil suit, which would be illegal on our end to do. That wasn't, of course, why we were doing it.

Trust me, I was filled with fear and anxiety and worry. My sister and I couldn't figure out what to do, and I could not sleep a wink. But we kept communicating about our conundrum, and we'd waited 24 hours before making a decision. (This is a great example of the 24-hour rule, by the way. Remember, when you're emotional, you're not rational—so never make a decision based on temporary feelings.)

We decided we'd fire Miss Psychopath Face—because it was the best decision for Dreamshine, and not one based on fear. Our clients, not fear, come first. It was a 10-month process costing us $20,000, but we did the right thing. Even when we met with Miss Psychopath Face through mediators and she continued to lie, overreacting and getting angry, we kept the fear away. Her true colors showed in that meeting. She got so angry that she basically started yelling at everyone in the entire room, including people who were there to represent her. Long story short, they dismissed the case, and it never even became an official civil suit—her claim was proven to be a full-blown lie.

Here's a very important question to ask yourself. As leaders and owners going through similar situations, what's best for your business overall? When I think about the big picture, it was a no-brainer. I knew not only was this best for Dreamshine, but also that there was no way we could allow Miss Psychopath Face back into our building when we knew she was stealing and filing a fraudulent civil suit against us.

When Fear Seeps through Social Media

My podcast, *Elevating Beyond*, has been up and running for five years. It just hit the five-year anniversary, which is amazing, and it's crazy that it has more than four million downloads across the world. But I'll never forget when one of my podcast connections (we'll call him Mr. Entitlement Face) just left me hanging in the wind. He said, "It's all yours—I'm just done." I thought: *Do I just stop the show now? Am I going to be able to keep it going? I haven't done it on my own yet.* Once again, I decided that I wasn't going to allow fear to drive me, and I would continue to move forward with the podcast.

This is a great time to remember your why. For my podcast, my "why" is always sharing the story behind the story of great people from all over the world who have overcome adversity to achieve significant success. Whether it's NFL players, Fortune 500 owners, *New York Times* best-selling authors or firefighters, I've had such a variety of people on my show. People have written to me, in emails and posts, saying: "I've been going through a really hard time. And I've even been having thoughts of suicide. And listening to your show has pushed me through this. I'm still not past it yet, but you helped me get out of a dark place." This is my "why"—I remember, dude, you don't get to give up.

Mr. Entitlement Face started pestering me about images of him on social media. I'd remove the images, but he'd keep emailing and texting me, even going as far as asking me to remove something from 30 episodes ago. I began panicking about the time it would take me, and realizing I was starting to make decisions based on fear. Social media can seem to have a strange power over us. But actually, it doesn't. You are the captain of your mindset. You can choose to set boundaries. You can choose what you want to read or not read, to reply or not reply. You can choose to block people.

But people like Mr. Entitlement Face can't hold you hostage. You have the right to freakin' cut them off and block them and free yourself from the fear. Cut those energy vampires out of your life. And that is exactly what I did. Mr. Entitlement Face gradually faded away, and *Elevating Beyond* has gone beyond my wildest dreams. It was another pivotal moment when I almost allowed fear to dictate my course of action. I love to be honest, vulnerable, and transparent, and I still go through this. It's not a one-and-done thing. Put it on your wall. Post it. It's one of our core values at Dreamshine: never make decisions based on fear.

Truth Bombs

- Fear is just a feeling. It can't physically stop you. Action alleviates fear. Inaction elevates fear.
- Everyone faces fear—even some of your favorite entrepreneurs and entertainers.
- Your purpose has to be greater than your fear.
- Never allow your ego to determine a decision.

- Never make a permanent decision based on temporary feelings. Give yourself 24 hours to make a decision based on the facts you have, and with a sound mind—not based on fear and emotion.
- The fear never goes away. It's up to you to get rid of it by taking action—not standing still. Each time you do this, you build your courage muscles more and more.

11

You Suck at Growing Trees: How and When to Branch Out in Your Business

Trees. That's right. We're talking about growing freakin' trees—as in, branching out your business. It's more complicated than you think, or it needs to be done in a different way than you think. Or . . . gosh, I'll just shut up. Now I'm overthinking this, making it way more over-freakin'-complicated than it needs to be. Let's move on.

I hear people say it all the time: "Every multimillionaire has at least five streams of income and blah blah blah." That may be true. I have multiple streams now, but remember, there's no "30 days to success," or any of that crap. I'm all for branching out into different areas. But there's different levels, and it takes more time than you think.

Let's admit it. Many of us are entrepreneurs, and we're really good at chasing those shiny objects, aren't we? We get bored with a tiny success, and we keep moving on to these tiny little successes, which never actually build anything. And believe me, I've been guilty of this myself. Sometimes we chase things we think would be a great idea, and it fails catastrophically. But failure is a chance to grow wisdom. Speaking of growing, here's how you grow trees the right way.

Start with the roots.

Pay attention to your company's foundation. Building that strong trunk takes time to grow that tree, to water that tree, so those roots can grow deeper and further into the ground. If you start branching out too quickly without having those deep roots you've built during the years from everything I've been teaching you in this book so far, it can look great for a season. It can be like, "Wow, that tree has 16 more branches, and it looks like it's growing so fast and quickly." But if you didn't take enough time to build the base and let those roots really dig deep and anchor into the foundation, the next season hits, snow falls, and guess what? Because that tree didn't have enough time to grow strong roots, the weight of the snow will cause it to collapse and topple over.

What it really takes is starting to prune some of the branches, which seems like the opposite of what you should do. But when you prune them, the roots are growing deeper and stronger. Then the tree starts blooming at a whole other level.

Love does grow a tree.

Money doesn't grow on trees, and it doesn't grow trees, either. In other words, branching out your business just for money will create rot. Learning to rediscover your purpose, meanwhile, will allow you to thrive as a leader, owner, or influencer for many years.

Just look at Bob Goff, author of *Love Does*, one of my favorite books. He calls himself "a recovering lawyer." Even though he was one of the good guys, suing companies that made crooked skyscrapers instead of defending crooks, he stopped thinking of law as a career. It wasn't his passion. But it could help fund his true purpose: working with kids in Uganda and India and, as he writes, "chasing bad guys who hurt them." After he started a nonprofit, he and his wife turned his law career into a strong tree so they could branch out. "Now, Sweet Maria and I think about my day job as a great way to fund the things we're doing," he writes. "Now when I put on a suit and tie or jump on a plane to go take a deposition, we call it 'fundraising.' It still makes me grin every time to say it this way. It's like a really successful bake sale to get rid of the bad guys."

You don't have to save kids in Africa to branch out the right way. I get it; you want to grow your company or your influence. But if you branch out too quickly, those twigs will get crushed by the next storm. That quick fix some offer through social media marketing, promising you six figures in a month? Sorry, but duct tape has no place on a tree. Love *does* grow a tree: love for yourself, your team, your company, and your community. Once you tap into that resource, you'll find branching out happens much more organically.

Sure, we still need money to make payroll, pay the building's rent, meet mortgage payments at home, and afford groceries. I've branched out and made different financial investments that have been huge failures. *Huge* failures. But I've also branched out and continually built things that have been incredible successes as well. What I have never done is jeopardize the whole tree.

Leveling Up

In case my tree metaphor stumps you a bit, I'm going to break it down with my own real-life example. Let's go back to our "why." I've mentioned how it has different levels, starting with the foundation. My "why" was to create the most amazing place in a beautiful, resort-like atmosphere with the most incredible options possible for individuals with developmental disabilities, unlike any other in Ohio. As we continued to build Dreamshine, about two years in, the next level was to become the best leader possible for my team, which is everything I've taught you. I've been walking you through that journey throughout this book, starting with me as the leader, the owner, to develop myself, and then inspiring and teaching my team to practice leadership and elevate and create amazing unity in the Dream Team.

When we were a few years in, with a solid tree trunk with deep roots, I was able to branch out toward my other passion for my *Elevating Beyond* podcast. I can share not only my story of overcoming adversity, but also have guests from all over the world sharing their stories. I also have my books and my speaking engagements. But the individuals whom we serve are always the foundation of everything I do.

And by the way, I'm still branching out with this book, which goes beyond having places hire me to speak. We're putting on our own live events, 16 Reasons Why Your Business Sucks, at our Dreamshine campus, and I invite you to attend. Amazing leaders and business owners will be doing freakin' awesome things for three days. You'll get to see my Dream Team in action. This also creates options for amazing individuals to be involved in these events.

I don't know if we've officially mentioned it to the public yet (as I write this), but the proceeds of *16 Reasons* are going toward Dreamshine. That's right—by purchasing this book, you're helping change the lives of the individuals we serve. We'll be able to add more to our program and pay our amazing Dream Team what they truly deserve. This is another example of how to take purpose and passion to another level.

Truth Bombs

- In order to grow a business, start with the roots—the company's foundation and core values.
- Avoid people offering a quick fix; duct tape has no place on a tree.

Never jeopardize the whole tree.

CHAPTER 12

You Suck at Firing: When, Why, and How to Fire Employees

Sugar coat it all you want. You have to "let people go." Whatever. We're talking about freakin' firing people from the team. It's not something sweet. It's not something fun.

But when you suck at firing, it destroys the unity of your team. When you're a coward, you bring down your organization. It's your job to make the harder decisions. Once I thought serving your team meant enabling everyone and trying to be the nice guy. But only by firing the toxic people on your team will you enhance the company.

The Full Story of Mr. Negative Face

You've heard about Mr. Negative Face, a Dreamshine employee, a couple of times in this book. Now, here's the full story, a slice of humble pie as I illustrated how much I sucked at firing people.

Mr. Negative Face was a neighbor's brother-in-law, and seemed like a great hire. Mr. Negative Face was *amazing* when working with our individuals with developmental disabilities. He was excellent at his job—Mr. Happy Face. But when he interacted with other team members, another side took over. He'd verbally lash out at fellow employees. It was explosive sometimes. He could be openly aggressive and passive-aggressive. It was uncomfortable, even more so because of our neighbors.

So we'd go through the cycles: Mr. Negative Face would blow up, I'd talk to him about the problem, he'd simmer down for a few weeks—even writing out apologies to employees—and then he'd start poking at everyone again. Every time we discussed resolving conflict, and every month, I'd see Mr. Negative Face causing conflict.

I sucked at it. I let the situation fester for three months, then six months, then 12 months—and before I knew it, Mr. Negative Face had been wreaking havoc on the team culture. Then one day, his out-burst was so bad—he was screaming at *everyone*, including my sister and me—we had to fire him. Finally. But I will never forget the night before, lying in bed and thinking out of fear, *What's going to happen when I fire him tomorrow?* I knew I had to, but what would he do? We were such a small company, what about the few people that were close to him? I was completely allowing fear to dictate all of my decisions and my thinking. And remember, we don't make decisions based on fear. But that's exactly what I was doing.

When we met and fired him the next day, it was the complete opposite of all of these fake fears that I was facing. Right there I made a note that *whoa!* as a leader I was a freakin' coward, and never again would I let myself make decisions based on fear. After we "let go" of Mr. Negative Face, we learned he'd been gossiping and spreading toxic rumors behind the scenes. It got to the point that he was com-pletely lying, and the gossip was so toxic it could have endangered the individuals with developmental disabilities lives that we are honored to serve. I'll explain this to you in detail and literally why we have adopted our no-gossip policy.

How Gossip Can Get Someone Fired

Gossip sounds like a silly little problem from a teen TV series, but for maintaining team morale and a successful company culture, it's a real big problem sometimes. One of our transportation vans had a faulty seat belt. Mr. Negative Face rode this van all the time, but never told me about the issue. For more than two months, he complained to fellow team members about the broken seat belt. I was, he gossiped, too cheap to fix it.

Are you freakin' kidding me? Too cheap to fix it? I never even knew the seat belt was broken. More than anything, I value the health and safety of the individuals with developmental disabilities.

When I found out about the seat belt, I fixed it right away, but the gossip had already done permanent damage by creating a subculture of distrust. His refusal to tell someone who could take action also endangered the lives of the individuals with disabilities we're honored to serve. This became much bigger than just about someone gossiping. This was about problems festering instead of getting fixed.

Our team members get one warning. We review the gossip, telling them how everyone makes mistakes, and we're always growing and learning. But our core values are nonnegotiable. If the gossip continues, we terminate the individual.

When people hear about our No-Gossip Policy at Dreamshine, they often ask to see an example. Rather than describing it repeatedly in one-on-one conversations, I decided to share it with everyone right here in this book.

Dreamshine No-Gossip Policy

If any Dreamshine team member is caught gossiping, they will be given one warning. Then if caught gossiping again, they will be terminated.

People who work on our team will at times have frustrations. Having continued growth and quality demands fixing something, problem-solving, and unity. However, gossip is negative, insidious, and terribly contagious. It only accelerates the problems that need to be eliminated. Dreamshine embraces unity; therefore, gossip is not tolerated.

Here are some examples of how to define gossip, so team members can avoid it. We know at times team members are going to encounter problems. What matters is how the problems are treated. Problems or gripes are fine, but they must be handed *up* to leadership. Problems or gripes that are handed down or laterally are by definition gossip and run the risk of the team member sharing it being fired.

Suppose a team member has ongoing struggles with his/her leader/supervisor. Although they may both be talented, they continue to clash. Then the team member makes the mistake of sharing his/her frustrations with a coworker, in which he/she was given a warning. However, following the warning, he/she decided to go on and share with two other people (either laterally or down as described above). He/she would then be fired.

Here is another hypothetical example: a team member whose computer was trash was trying to process orders. You see, IT had done a poor job of getting it fixed or replaced, so the team member did have a legitimate gripe. But the team member made the mistake of sitting with the receptionist and venting for 15 minutes as to how management didn't care, and IT was incompetent, and asking how could the owners let this go on. The receptionist has never fixed a computer or budgeted to replace a computer, so the receptionist could do nothing to help. This is gossip. If the team member wants their computer to be fixed, they need to discuss this with someone who can make that happen.

*Again, hand your negatives up and your positives down. Otherwise, it is gossip.

Leaders, however, must respect the importance of not reprimanding a team member in front of other people. This in itself violates a basic rule of leadership.

Dreamshine is proud to be an awesome, unified team, embracing the innovative values of what our organization stands for. Dreamshine's awesome environment values positive peer pressure, created by a "gossip-free zone" culture where Dreams shine on!

I have to give credit and a shout out to my good man Dave Ramsey and his team, who told me about their company's no-gossip policy when I attended a leadership seminar in 2012.

Watch out for the leaky tire people.

These are some of the trickiest freakin' team members to deal with.

You're driving your car, and the tire pressure indicator lights up. When you check the tires, one seems a little lower than the others, so you fill it with air. It still leaks, but you're able to patch it. You're driving, and everything seems to be working great, and boom! Something's off. The tire pressure indicator lights up again. You pull over and realize your tire is leaking again, but now in a different spot. So you patch that area, and you drive again. Once again, it's leaking, this time, you see, a little bit in a bunch of different areas. You keep patching the tire, but now it's unpredictable and possibly risky, too. Plus it's also seriously freakin' annoying.

Which brings me back to the real-life example of someone we now call Mr. Leaky Tire Face. He was a really good guy, but something was just off. I remembered Dave Ramsey asking our seminar about such team members: "If the same person were to come back, knowing everything you know today, would you still hire them?"

My answer is, "Oh my gosh, no! No!" As I look through the documentation, I realized Mr. Leaky Tire Face had been written up like 200 different times over the past years, but each time for a freakin' different thing! I fired him, and of course, it was hard as he was and is a very nice guy, but we immediately saw how much better the Dreamshine "vehicle" ran the moment he was gone. Get rid of the leaky tire people.

Phenomenal attracts phenomenal: eagles and turkeys

We can also look at this one with turkeys and eagles. The eagles are your top performers; they're soaring up high, helping to push your company to new levels. The turkeys are the ones wobbling and gobbling around, wasting time pecking around in the land of mediocrity.

The eagles just want to soar. One of our core values at Dreamshine is S.O.A.R.—serve others abundantly and restlessly. We've built a culture of eagles, and we even include that in the job description. In our hiring process, we do everything we can to weed out any turkeys. But sometimes, turkeys make their way into Dreamshine. Or, sadly, we've had some people who are eagles at the start but down the line start turning into turkeys. As a leader, it's important that you are continuing to check in with them and work with them. If these turkeys aren't willing to change and elevate and soar like eagles, you need to get rid of them. Because you might have eleven team members but only eight eagles, and those turkeys could chase the eagles away. Now you have a culture of turkeys attracting turkeys, when you should have a culture of eagles attracting eagles who want to soar. Mediocre attracts mediocre, but phenomenal also attracts phenomenal.

Get rid of those turkeys, and continue to make eagles the new normal on your Dream Team. Notice how they might be impacting other team members' performance. The eagles, meanwhile, can be attracting other eagles to join them, either as new employees or as fellow employees elevating beyond their previous limits.

The 90-day probationary period

As I've discussed earlier in this book, we go through a very long hiring process before we even bring someone on. But still, what we've learned is that 90 days just helps us give another time frame. It gets us a little past that honeymoon phase to see if people really are the eagles that they presented themselves to be. And you know what? We've had some situations where people came on and truly were great. But during the 90-day probationary period, we've been able to realize that others weren't a good fit for us, and we weren't a good fit for them. We've been able to have a great conversation. For them also, it's often a relief where they'll say, "I love you guys, I love everything you're doing. This just is different than I expected." It's not like they're leaving on bad terms.

When a Dream Team member does hit the end of their 90-day probationary period, we always have a special ritual at our monthly all-Dream Team meeting where everyone celebrates and claps for them, and they get their official Dreamshine T-shirt. It's freakin' awesome, by the way, and serves as a rite of passage. They're also awarded some goodies, which we'll talk about in Chapter 14.

Pulling weeds and wasting fertilizer

Remember Mr. Leaky Tire Face? On the flip side of this is a great dude I knew who we'll call Mr. Fertilizer Face (in a good way!). He'd moved up the ladder over the years but was in a position that was more administrative, with more paperwork, not in his zone of genius and strength. In our "garden" of business, he wasn't a weed we should pull. He was willing to grow. We were just wasting fertilizer in the wrong place. It came to light that he had an amazing strength in working the floor, working directly with the clients and team members. We were able to use that fertilizer in another part of the garden.

It's another example of continuing to create massive levels of unity among our team members. Mr. Fertilizer Face showed so much appreciation, knowing that we as leadership took the time to work with him and find a place for his superpowers. This is our job as leaders, to position others where they can grow.

Explain the "why" behind the firing.

It's unkind to be unclear. At Dreamshine, when someone is fired, they shouldn't be caught by surprise. And let me explain what I mean by this. We would have met with this team member several times, giving them a chance and telling them this is how we do it. We might say, "You're doing awesome here, but something needs to change." You don't beat around the bush. We have nice, grown-up conversations, and we've had a lot of amazing team members who have continued to grow and elevate. When there's no sign of change, you sit with them for a final time. And you explain the exact reason behind the firing, which correlates to our core values.

This also ties to our core value of not allowing a conflict to go unresolved. Your job as a leader is to be continually working with them. Don't wait for some stupid annual review and tell them all these things are wrong. We don't do that. Again, when they don't improve within a reasonable time, you need to fire them.

It's time to share with you a real-life example—Ms. Always 10 Minutes Late Face. She was freakin' awesome at everything except being on time. And we had to address the situation seriously. She was continuously 10, 15, or 20 minutes late, which had a big impact on our process.

Here's where we explain the reason behind it because another part of our services is providing transportation to our different individuals with developmental disabilities whom we pick up and drop off each day. We have a transportation coordinator, and every pick up window is calculated and planned. We run 10 different routes. Everything's so planned that if you're just 5 or 10 minutes off, you can hit the huge rush of traffic coming into Columbus, which can delay everything by 30 minutes. The individuals we serve miss out on our programming, and their parents and families are late for their jobs.

When this happened with Ms. Always 10 Minutes Late Face, a leader met with her and addressed it dead on, explaining the reason everyone must arrive on time. Timeliness wasn't just an arbitrary rule.

She totally got it; she apologized and then was doing great for about another two weeks. And then it happened again, where she was about 15 minutes late. The leader immediately met with her, explaining how the seriousness of the situation was rising to another level. It wasn't fair to the other Dream Team members, who were showing up on time, or actually even early. (Another team member struggling with this literally sets four different alarms to make sure they're awake and at Dreamshine 10 to 15 minutes early.)

In all honesty, we met with Ms. Always 10 Minutes Late Face four times. The last time, we told her that if she ever showed up late again without a serious emergency, she'd be choosing to fire herself and would have to turn in her keys.

Well, guess what? It was about two days later that Ms. Always 10 Minutes Late Face showed up 10 minutes late, again. She chose to fire herself. She packed up her belongings, turned in her keys, and left.

It's so important, out of respect, to explain the reason behind something. Otherwise people can't connect all the dots, and that's wrong. That needs to change.

Explaining the "why" earns respect and can have very positive effects, too. Because after Ms. Always 10 Minutes Late Face fired herself, she sent a freakin' thank-you letter—genuinely, not sarcastically, seriously—to the entire Dream Team for helping build her character. She opened up and shared her respect for all the team members and apologized to everyone, saying she was so sorry she'd let everyone down. It really made her look back and reflect that this had been a lack-of-character issue her whole life. She'd always been late, and that was the wake-up call for her to make a real change. She owned it. What a blessing.

You won't believe that over the years, we've actually received thank-you letters from different team members we fired or had fire themselves. Now, don't get me wrong; we've had plenty of other ones who were like Miss Psychopath Face, who just said a bunch of horrible things. But that goes with the territory.

Truth Bombs

- It's your obligation as a leader to make the hard decisions and fire people who aren't a good fit. This is how you serve the team!
- It's unkind to be unclear.
- If team members aren't willing or equipped to grow, you need to let them go.
- Ask yourself, "If that same person were to come back and apply for the same position today, and you knew everything you now know about them, would you hire them again?"
- Watch out for the gossips, the leaky tires, and the turkeys— anyone who fails to adhere to your core values.

CHAPTER 13

You Suck at Subcontractors

I almost didn't write this chapter. Lucky freaking you. But I've continued to realize the importance of this, through my own experiences and from having so many different discussions at my speaking events, through my podcasts, and with business owners. As your business continues to grow, you will absolutely be working with more and different subcontractors, some for different seasons that you're in, and some for the longer term. Some might be accountants, payroll companies, web developers, podcast editors, publishers, subcontractors working on renovations—you name it. But what I've been hearing more and more from talking to a lot of you is an increase of horror stories of how people have gotten screwed over and how things have gone really bad with subcontractors. And believe me, I've learned some of these lessons the very hard way myself. I've also learned how to have amazing relationships with different subcontractors.

So here are the eight commandments to help you learn how not to suck at subcontractors.

1. Check references. No, really, check references.

Seems like a no-brainer, but you'd be surprised how many people suck at checking references—myself included. Years ago at Dreamshine, we worked with a CPA firm we had heard about in passing. No real check of their credentials, and we paid their pretty expensive rates for four years. They did a *pretty* good job with our accounting, but over time, more and more important errors were bubbling up. For example, we were implementing an expensive health plan for our employees. It was $80,000, a big chunk of change for us, but we were very excited.

Lo and be-freaking-hold, the firm failed to put the plan into our company taxes. Because of interest and other charges from this error, I had to pay $24,000 in additional taxes out of my pocket. You can imagine I was pretty freakin' upset about this, but mistakes happen, and everyone has to be part of the team, including subcontractors. But in this case, they sucked at taking accountability. To top it off, they even billed us for the time to fix their own errors, which were already costing us all that money and all the additional taxes they were supposed to be freakin' helping us with. It was a freaking nightmare.

Because we'd been with the firm for more than five years, I started feeling fear about switching to a new accounting firm that didn't know us. But then I realized, boom! We don't make decisions based on fear. Just like anything else, if subcontractors aren't working out, ask yourself what's best for the company. You need to fire them if they aren't freakin' awesome. It's a short-term inconvenience, but it's absolutely the best thing to do for your company in the long run.

As we switched to a different CPA, I approached the process differently. We had narrowed it down to two companies, and I made sure to do the following:

- Get references I could contact right away.
- Interview the CPAs.
- Ask for a test run of their services.

One company checked out really well in the reference check, offered to fly from Chicago to meet with us, and allowed us to try their services for a month. The other company we weeded out very quickly, because they wouldn't even give out references to begin with—they were actually offended by the question. Always check the references! If they're not willing to give them, bye! See you later! Find someone else.

2. Beware of anyone who promises a short-term fix.

Let's say you have video courses, and a subcontractor offers "click funnels." In 30 days, they say, you'll be making six figures per month. I get it. You're tired, you're exhausted. You're working so many different levels here as a business owner and as an entrepreneur, and you want someone to take this weight off your shoulders. You're hoping it pans out. But, in the long run, they screw you over, so you lose money, waste your time, and end up worse off than you were when you began. Remember the old saying, if it's too good to be true, then it probably is too good to be true.

3. Do not pay the subcontractor full until the job is freakin' finished.

Again, I've learned this the hard way. I can't even remember the number of times a subcontractor at Dreamshine has left holes in the drywall, or failed to finish a pipe project, or walked out on a website redesign. One subcontractor even stood us up and left the state! The list goes on and on. Establish clear terms from the start. You could do 50% upfront, 25% when the finish line is in sight and the last 25% when the job is done and you've confirmed it to *your* satisfaction.

We spent four months wasting our time and energy on finishing a sloppy job. Repeat after me: nobody gets the full 100% until you're 100% satisfied. And don't be afraid to change the game. We recently worked with a payroll company and changed their standard implementation practice to match our needs. They said, "We have more than 5,000 clients and no one has ever done this in the history of blah blah blah." Again, *great*! I'm used to being the first one to do something! And I know you are, too, because you're an entrepreneur. You're a leader. You're used to being the one going into that uncharted territory.

For example, with this payroll company. They're getting money from you. You're hiring them. You're paying them for services. If they're not confident they will do it 100% to awesomeness, then screw them and move onward.

And by the way, I've learned something funny in those situations where you don't make that final payment until it's 100% done to your satisfaction. I've had those same people who left the holes in the drywall where it took months of calling them to fix it. But when I reminded them I still owed that last 25%, they were magically able to be out there literally the same day to finish fixing the holes to our satisfaction.

4. Never, ever, ever allow subcontractors to hold you hostage.

Here's another fun little subcontractor adventure for you. I'd hired a company to redo our website, and they did a great job! But I had been sucked into their services on their terms. So when we needed updates or had problems, they were charging double the price. Total crap. Basically, the website company was holding me hostage, since they owned all the services. Now, I have a different process for my two websites (one for Dreamshine, one for Mark Minard) and my *Elevating Beyond* site: using a third-party host with my own password. Nobody can hold me hostage now.

5. Handle subcontractor conflict as you would with your team members.

I've been telling you about our amazing waterfront lodge project at Dreamshine: new colors, a living wall of plants, a store, and even a kitchen where we'll host our cooking show. We also have these multi-sensory rooms, which a subcontractor completely messed up as I was writing this book. I'd been working with him for about two years, but the finalization did *not* turn out the way it was supposed to. I was so upset, I broke one of my own rules: **don't text conflict**. And then another: **wait 24 hours to allow yourself to calm down**. I immediately sent a half-page long text.

What a freaking moron I was! And guess what? This created even more conflict—a blowup. If I'd only followed the same approach I do with my team members, the situation would have settled down right away. Fortunately, we were able to get it all worked out. And we have a great relationship. But this ended up adding more time and more drama, which was my fault. And I took accountability for that, even though they needed to make the fixes. Lesson learned. Sometimes I get punched in the face, as we all do as leaders. So remember, for goodness' sake, that subcontractors work with you; they're an extension of your team. You always want to continue to keep creating that unity, which leads to that unstoppable, powerful force of momentum.

6. When a subcontractor does something super freakin' awesome, reward them in a super freakin' awesome way!

At Dreamshine, we bill some clients through the state Medicaid and Medicare programs, which can get backed up in the county billing departments. One woman, though, was one of the few people in the entire state of Ohio to actually be polite and thorough in getting the job done. It was so refreshing to continually see this. This was so huge because as we work with the different counties in the state for the billing, there's times where they can owe us more than $30,000 in claims. Furthermore, we've had to fight sometimes for months to get those.

It was so refreshing to continually see her doing this the right way, delivering on a whole new level. She always was there to help us with anything in our building and even get people quickly connected to others, with no ulterior motive.

One day, it just made me think, "Man! She's so awesome." I was so grateful, I sent her a bouquet of roses and a card: "Thank you so much from Mark Minard at Dreamshine for how awesome you are and always over-delivering." It was the same way we reward our team members when they're being awesome. She wrote back saying in 20 years of working with the county, no one had ever done anything like that. The little things make a big difference

7. Always have options.

Remember, once again, there is always another way. Continue to create options. I have a lot of payroll stories, but here's another one. When I discovered some potential new benefits for our team, our payroll company refused to switch our program. To sum it up, I had a 401(k) for them, and I learned through research that by switching to a simple IRA for our company setup, I'd have more funds available for paying less in admin fees, and I'd actually be able to match what my team members put in at a higher percentage, giving them even more benefits. Unfortunately, the payroll company wasn't open to creating any other options and acted like it was only A or B.

Don't ever let anyone put you in a freakin' only A or B scenario. And by the way, as a subcontractor, that's stupid. That's how you lose business. There's always a C, D, E, F, G, all the way through Z. They could have made a way to work with us and switch it over. And even though we wouldn't be doing that part of the 401(k) for them (and they were probably making money off the admin fees), they still would have continued to have us as a client and make money off the payroll. But again, they tried to threaten us into this A/B thing. Don't let anyone do that. Start looking for other options immediately. You can bring those back to the subcontractor and offer them a chance to match. If not? "See you later." Again, the key to your leverage is to always create options. It takes a little more work in the short term, but in the long term, it will be so much better for the business as a whole. Just remember, always have options.

8. Good does not freakin' equal great.

We had a good insurance company (let's call it Company A) for many years at Dreamshine. I knew the owner, and he was a nice guy. They were good. Then we added more transportation services, and our vehicle insurance for the company went from $2,000 a month to nearly $9,000 a month. We explained that we couldn't afford it. We needed to find something better. It was insanity. Company A came up with a better offer, but not much better. I found Company B, a specialist in vehicle insurance for our industry, which was able to get the same coverage much closer to $2,000 a month than $9,000. We switched from the nice guy's Company A—which was good but not great—to Company B, and we've been with them ever since.

14

You Suck at Giving Trophies: Rewarding Performance and Giving Raises the Right Way

G eneric annual reviews. Generic annual raises. It's a freaking stupid corporate process that's gone on for far too long. Check the boxes, and everyone gets a trophy. How about actual performance and attitude? Here are some much more creative ways to calculate and give awesome bonuses, incentives, and raises.

Calculating pay and Bonuses

Let's just get straight to the point about raises. Mediocre companies *only* factor in time. Yes, time is important, and we value loyalty. but at Dreamshine we also factor in attitude and performance. In fact, we use this formula: 50% Time + 25% Performance + 25% Attitude. The job's responsibilities are the foundation, and the greater the responsibilities, the bigger the problems and the higher the pay scale. But the formula remains the same. I also love Christmas bonuses and rely on our trusty formula to give our Dream Team members something extra at that time of year.

Job performance doesn't operate on a calendar.

So why should you? Annual, generic job performance reviews suck. When we're having an issue with someone at Dreamshine, we don't wait a freaking year to address it. So be the great leader you are, and address it immediately. If you have any questions, go back to Chapter 3, Why You Suck at Conflict. It's unkind to be unclear, so it's an ongoing process of teaching, elevating, and communicating. The same goes for raises: no trophy mentality. Two people might hold the exact same position and have different pay rates because one works harder and has a better attitude. Rewarding someone who's not pulling their weight is just ridiculous. Stop doing annual forms as a way to procrastinate. Help your amazing and willing team members to grow to that next level.

Dispense tokens of awesomeness.

You know those old-school claw machines where 50 cents gets you a try at grabbing a stuffed animal. One day, I came across a miniature version on Amazon and grabbed it for about $30; it's now officially known as the Dreamshine Token of Awesomeness machine. But instead of stuffed animals, it's filled with cash: $5, $10, $20; we even slip in a couple $50 bills each month. When a Dream Team member is caught doing something awesome, they get Token of Awesomeness. Everyone cheers them on, and they win money. What I love is that our Dream Team has gotten so laser-focused and skilled, they have it down to a science where it will grab three or four bills at a time. It's become such a foundational part of our culture at Dreamshine.

We literally have a monthly budget set for cash for our Token of Awesomeness machine.

Another secret little thing we do happens when new Dream Team members are filling out their new-hire information. We slip in a little piece of paper (which they usually forget about), asking about their favorite restaurants, hobbies, soft drinks, snacks. What makes this awesome? It's a really cool way to reward team members creatively in a way that shows you're really thinking about them and caring about them.

Remember how I also mentioned at the end of the 90-day probationary period we have, when everyone claps for them at the all-Dream Team meeting? It's a rite of passage, and they're given their official Dreamshine T-shirt and other cool things. This is a perfect example of when we would slide in there something like one of their favorite drinks, which might be a Diet Pepsi. And we saw that they listed their favorite kind of snack is Cool Ranch Doritos. They get that on top of everything else. They're like, "Oh my gosh, how the heck did you know?" They light up: "Diet Pepsi! That's my favorite drink. And Cool Ranch Doritos. These are my favorite chips!" They don't even remember that they ever filled out that form, which makes it so fun and cool. It's just another super great way to go above and beyond.

Flex your creativity muscles. Show me the results in all the cool ways you recognize your team members. Tag me on social media, and I'll tag you back with pictures and videos of Dreamshine—even someone winning $50 at the Token of Awesomeness machine! (Or maybe I'll even surprise you with your own Cool Ranch Doritos 😊)

Rewarding in Different Ways

It doesn't have to be money, food, or even anything tangible. A job's rewards should be learning how to push and challenge yourself in amazing ways, no matter your level in the company. For our monthly all-Dream Team meetings, I always find a cool motivational type clip that we share that's usually like three to five minutes long. One of them that's been a regular is Eric Thomas. Look him up. Eric Thomas, ET, the hip-hop preacher. He's one of the top motivational speakers in the world. I freakin' love him. Seriously, just type in Eric Thomas on YouTube, and you'll see one of his videos has more than 50 million views. We share it at our all-Dream Team Meetings.

This is a great example of how you need to always innovate in different ways. When I found the passion to start my podcast, *Elevating Beyond*, on top of Dreamshine, I thought it was crazy at the time. But as you push through, taking action leads to new discoveries you could never imagine. And throughout the years of having my podcast and having different guests from all over the world, I got to personally get to know and have Eric Thomas on my show. Through a series of events, I was able to work with him and even be able to get him to personally come out and speak to my company, Dreamshine, which we arranged as a private event just for the Dream Team and family members (about 25 people). The fact that it normally costs up to $100,000, (Seriously, that's his speaking fee. He's the man!) and we were able to make special arrangements to get him to come, spend time, and speak at Dreamshine? I don't know what else to say. It was mind blowing.

These are things you can do at a whole other creative level. Don't be afraid to try new things. Don't worry about looking stupid when you're trying to do cool things for your team. You always have to innovate to elevate.

Truth Bombs

- Mediocre companies *only* factor in time. Great companies factor in time, attitude, and performance.
- Don't wait for generic, annual performance reviews; spend the time helping your team members grow and innovate to the next level **ongoing**.
- You have to innovate to elevate.

15

You Suck at Self: Self-Awareness, Self-Accountability, & Self-Confidence

L isten up, ladies and gentlemen. We hear the talk all of the time: self-awareness this, self-awareness that. Self-accountability, self-confidence, blah, blah, blah.

You know why? Because it's true! Choosing to learn these traits will make you awesome. Choosing not to practice these traits will make you suck.

Let's take a look at customer service. Recently, my wife and I took our family to the Columbus Zoo, which has a cool waterpark connected to it. I hope they take notes and apply what I'm about to share with you. It was mid-July, a 90-degree, hot, humid day. We had our three children with us, along with three of their friends, ranging from ages 5–11. We were excited to be there, but it was hot, sticky chaos, and we wanted to hit the waterpark right away.

But we knew to prepare in advance, ordering tickets online and reading the rules that we could bring our own cooler, as long as it was the right size, with our own food and drinks. There we were, standing in line to enter, and the attendant said in a lethargic, sarcastic, rude, and irritated tone, "Uh, you can't bring coolers in here."

My wife showed him the note from the zoo's website about acceptable coolers. He said: "Oh, we're not connected online. We don't get the same updates that the zoo does because they have a separate website." You can see what was going on here: this employee was making their problem our problem.

A bunch of other families behind us also had coolers and started demanding an explanation. So now, the negativity was adding to the oppressive weather. The manager eventually showed up, and his attitude was even worse. We all ended up having to take our coolers back to our cars! Freaking ridiculous!

Yes, this was the waterpark connected to the Columbus Zoo, and it's a business, an organization. It could be you. This is why you must understand as a leader, it's on you to take action and accountability, to change such a sucky culture.

Imagine how different your approach could be:

"Oh, gosh—I see the proof that you just showed me regarding the coolers. Unfortunately, we're having an issue right now with our website not matching up with the zoo's website. I'm so sorry. You're not going to be able to bring those in, and I'm so sorry about it. Let me give you a $20 immediate coupon that you can go in and use in our gift shop to buy drinks, snacks, etc., and I'm going to find someone, and we're going to personally help you get those coolers back to your cars, and we're going to get you right in. I'm so sorry this happened."

Amazing! You've built a culture of empowerment where employees are able to take the initiative to solve situations on their own. Problems arise as you grow and develop. But it's better to tackle them and start fixing them right away, with a thankful mindset that you caught the mistake before more issues arose. Am I likely to recommend going to the waterpark after an experience like that? Nope, and

I *love* the Columbus Zoo. This is what happens when you fail to practice accountability.

P. S. Someone please send them a copy of this freakin' book. They totally need it.

Accountability in action

You've heard about our amazing waterfront lodge at Dreamshine. Just about everything was in place when one of our clients' moms expressed concern over the noise level. If I'd let stupid ego take over, I would have told her everything was perfect, while feeling annoyed. *How dare she question me?* Instead, I practiced accountability and realized she was right! We came up with some colorful, creative ways to install soundproofing. I also went back to the mom to thank her and apologized we hadn't already realized how high the noise level was.

That's why Dreamshine is the best. That's why we have a wait-list for individuals with developmental disabilities to come to our program. It starts with this mentality—this mindset of taking on accountability in a way where you drop your ego to look at the bigger picture. How can we fix this problem? How can we make this better? How can *I* make this better? Overdeliver. Make it freaking better, and always overdeliver.

Self-Awareness

No more excuses, OK? Excuses suck, and they don't fix the freaking problem. You fix problems. We fix problems. That's what we *do*. I'll be honest: I've been freaking *struggling* to finish this book. It's been a three-year project, and I love all the content, and I know my passion is going to help so many people. But I'm more of a speaker than a writer, not to mention the bazillion other things I have going on. I'm running my company, my podcast, speaking engagements all over; plus I have my five children and my wife. This is where you have to combine that self-awareness with accountability plus action. So, I'm practicing self-awareness by setting strict deadlines for myself as I'm writing this write now. I even booked a hotel room just up the street from my house, locking myself in this room for the next 24 hours to make sure I finish this chapter, and the next one. I let my assistant know I should not have any interruptions and to have very strict boundaries during this time. I'm not leaving until I'm done.

Self-Confidence

When people say, "You were born with self-confidence," it makes me cringe. No way. I struggle with more doubt and anxiety than the normal person. I openly talk about the panic attacks that I've had, and I'm proof that self-confidence is freaking muscle you continually can build. When you drop your ego, increase your self-awareness, and take accountability, that muscle will grow stronger and stronger.

It's just like working out; you start hitting the gym, and you look in the mirror, but you see no results. Then, after 30, 60, 90 days—whatever it takes—you *do* start seeing some results, which builds your confidence. Start skipping the gym to binge on Netflix and Cool Ranch Doritos? You get weak again. Keep working on that self-confidence; it's a lifelong exercise. Also, self-confidence is *not* arrogance or having a big ego. It's connected to your bigger "why" and continually having the courage to be yourself. To believe in your dreams. To know it's not about you. It's bigger than you. Those driven by their ego are focused on what makes them look good. At the foundation of ego is fear, and they lack self-confidence because they're always more worried about trying to prove their reputation and make themselves look good to others.

A great example of this comes from a movie that I love called *White Men Can't Jump*. Woody Harrelson teams up with Wesley Snipes, and they have a con playing basketball, hustling people for money, playing on the corner by the beach. And Woody Harrelson looks like this white dude who just sucks. So people are always betting against him. But Woody Harrelson actually is really good. He's not as flashy as Wesley Snipes. At one point, they get into an argument, and Harrelson says, "you would rather look good and lose than look bad and win." Those that are driven by their ego are only concerned and focused on what makes them look good versus a team winning as a whole. Make sure that you get rid of those people who are ego-driven. You're sabotaging your business. Return to building a freakin' awesome dream team culture. And for God's sake, if this is you right now, it's never too late to start changing. Start changing now.

The moment when Dave Ramsey punched me in the face.

Well, not really, but I'll never forget when he told me and 40 other business owners that *we* were entirely accountable for any company problems. The moment you have that realization, he explained, you get to be the solution. And boy, did this sucker punch come at just the right time. Back at Dreamshine, our new waterfront lodge was stressing our team out, causing delay after delay. My natural instinct was to blame the builder and subcontractors. After all, it truly was their fault as they had guaranteed the deadline. I had done everything possible on my end, but they'd be two months behind. Ramsey's words reminded me a real leader serves and takes massive accountability. It's weird because the voices in my head will tell me, *This is gonna make me look weak*, or *It's going to make me look like I'm not a good leader*, and it's the exact opposite.

I turned on my two-way radio for everyone on the Dream Team to hear: "We're going to be pushed back by two months, and we're going to come together for some creative solutions, but this is on me, and I'm so sorry." Instantly doing this shifted the whole tone of the atmosphere from stressed and irritable to positive and unified. Later, one of the Dream Team members approached me to share his respect and appreciation for my accountability.

This continues to be a regular part of our team culture where we'll see other team members step up and take accountability in front of the whole team in areas just like this.

The action is continuing to push you out of your comfort zone ongoing until the next level becomes normal for you. There's always another level! As you do these things, this is what creates that amazing culture, which elevates unity. Unity is one of the most powerful things that we can't even measure. Unity leads to one of my favorite words: momentum.

Truth Bombs

- Self-awareness + accountability + action = confidence.
- Drop the freaking ego.
- Humility comes before honor.
- Push yourself out of the comfort zone until the next level becomes normal for you.

16

You Suck at Perseverance: Elevating Beyond Fear, Doubt, and Anxiety

I've read dozens of great business and leadership books, and just when I feel equipped with the right tools, they push me out the door missing one critical step: how to persevere. How to elevate beyond your fear, doubt, and anxiety. I've had all three of these to exponential degrees. As you've been reading this book, I've been sharing my own true stories—the good, the bad, and the ugly from the past 13 years. But what's also really important to know is that I almost gave up on this book so many times.

For starters, I worked on this book for more than 18 months with a different editing and publishing team making video courses and so much more. They ended up totally screwing me more than halfway through the project and then immediately filing for bankruptcy, leaving the country with the $20,000 I'd invested in all this, not to mention all my time. What I'm going to share with you is how I continue and how you will continue to persevere beyond these things and keep taking action.

Now that I've regained my voice (have you counted how many times I've used the word freakin'?), I thought something really cool for this last chapter would be to open up, conversation-style, with you. I asked Cierra, one of my team members whom I've worked with for some time throughout this project, to interview me about perseverance and how I use it to elevate to another level beyond my fear, doubt, and anxiety—and how it can do the same for you, too.

Cierra: "Mark, when you first started this project, you were working with other people that you had ongoing problems with, which continued to make this drag on for more than three years. Did you ever think, *Man, maybe this just isn't the right time, or maybe I should just table this project*? What did it take to push through the process and say 'no matter what,' even with everything that's going on with Dreamshine, with all of the ups and downs that you continue to have while creating this book? So many times it would have been justified for you to just give up!"

Mark: "Yes! But it pushes you to a new level, out of your comfort zone. You're opening up. You're choosing to be really vulnerable. As you keep pushing yourself, you have internal and external challenges that will kind of start blindsiding you left and right with doubts. But this is not about me—it's about growing and developing other leaders, and I've already seen the impact of teaching it to my team and other companies. That's what keeps me going.

"I'd be lying if I said I don't feel fear. And then the imposter syndrome kicks in, that voice that says, 'Oh, you're not good enough to manage this, and you're a fake and a fraud.' But I tap back into my 'why.' I leave the pity party. Thank you, imposter syndrome; thank you, fear; thank you, doubt; you just proved that I'm going to push through it and that I'm going to get to a whole new level. Keep going! Freakin' onward and upward!"

Cierra: "When you go through all of these different levels of adversity and frustration—the different battles—what are some things that you actually do in the moment on those days to restart or to keep going throughout those times that other people can tangibly start doing? Can you share those with us?"

Mark: "Well, I do a variety of things. In my Dreamshine office and the *Elevating Beyond* studio, I hang tons of pictures of my family and so many other moments, and motivational quotes to remind me of my 'why.' Like Winston Churchill's: "Never, never, never quit." That one's special because it came from my good man Tim, who's in the U. S. Air Force and gave me a special leadership award. Also thank-you cards from team members and families. When I don't want to get out of bed in the morning, when I'm so beat down going through such a huge storm, I get a pad and paper and wake up and write down four things I'm grateful for. Sometimes it's as simple as a roof over my head, or being blessed to have business problems, because it means I own a company. The list grows longer as I drive to the studio or Dreamshine office. All day, I'm listening to YouTube videos and books on Audible to put me in a positive mindset. I've got my Airpods in, or I'm listening in my car without even watching the videos. Hey, I never said I was freakin' normal. Do you! At the end of the day, I add four more things to the list—and before I know it, I'm going to bed feeling much better about the next day.

Cierra: "I've noticed that there's a lot of talk lately about entre-preneurs, especially those who have been at it for quite a while, such as how to properly take care of themselves from a mental standpoint, so what do you do to make sure you stay healthy mentally and physi-cally, and in your relationships? How do you deal with all of this while you're changing the world?"

Mark: "Actually, I was just meeting with a business owner last night, and he's built an incredibly successful business, but he lost his marriage along the way. As I've written, it's important to pay attention to the seasons. You've gotta give up to go up, but that doesn't mean giving up on your health and getting so obese you have a heart attack, or just throwing your marriage out the window. What's the point? For relationships, it comes down to communication. I'm able to work on my health, for example, by communicating with my wife about a different schedule for the season, when I'll wake up at 4:30 a.m. to run and start working, and then be able to be home by 6 p.m. for the kids. Or I'll go for a quick jog around the Dreamshine neighborhood, and use baby wipes to freshen up for a meeting. You just have to keep figuring ways out to get through the different seasons that you're in. Something is always better than nothing. And if you want to just veg out and watch Netflix or football all day, go for it. Just be intentional about how it fits into your particular season.

"I love what my good man Ken Coleman, who was a guest on my podcast, told me about how Condoleezza Rice and other great leaders whom he's personally spent time with manage everything. The number-one thing he told me they all have in common is a lifelong pursuit of epic curiosity. 'They're always willing to learn,' he said. 'They're always curious to learn more.' And that's really what this is all about. Combine that perseverance with that epic curiosity. And drop your ego. Be willing to grow. Keep challenging yourself to grow, and know there's always another way. Stay epically curious."

Cierra: "Mark, is there anything else you'd like to add?"

Mark: "Being the leader is a lonely island. People think, *Well, Mark doesn't go through this anymore. He doesn't have depression or fear or anxiety, not like the way I do. He couldn't be speaking in front of thousands of people and lead his team, and writing these books.* And the thing is, Yes, I still do! It's not just you. When you have thoughts of depression and anxiety, it doesn't make you abnormal; it makes you a human being. You have to keep pushing through it one day, one step at a time. That's really what it is: perseverance. Find other like-minded people who have big visions and dreams like you, whom you can open up to. And to everyone reading this, you can push through anything to get to the next level. It's OK to feel your emotions. Just let it help you elevate beyond all the freaking crap!"

Truth Bombs

- Never, never, never quit.
- Stay epically curious.
- Freakin' onward and upward!

CONCLUSION

I have to end this book by sharing with you one of my favorite poems, which sums up everything about leadership and going after your dreams, your purpose . . .

It's called "If" By Rudyard Kipling

If you can keep your head when all about you
    Are losing theirs and blaming it on you,
If you can trust yourself when all men doubt you,
    But make allowance for their doubting too;
If you can wait and not be tired by waiting,
    Or being lied about, don't deal in lies,
Or being hated, don't give way to hating,
    And yet don't look too good, nor talk too wise:
If you can dream—and not make dreams your master;
    If you can think—and not make thoughts your aim;
If you can meet with Triumph and Disaster
    And treat those two impostors just the same;
If you can bear to hear the truth you've spoken
    Twisted by knaves to make a trap for fools,
Or watch the things you gave your life to, broken,
    And stoop and build 'em up with worn-out tools:
If you can make one heap of all your winnings
    And risk it on one turn of pitch-and-toss,

And lose, and start again at your beginnings
    And never breathe a word about your loss;
If you can force your heart and nerve and sinew
    To serve your turn long after they are gone,
And so hold on when there is nothing in you
    Except the Will which says to them: 'Hold on!'
If you can talk with crowds and keep your virtue,
    Or walk with Kings—nor lose the common touch,
If neither foes nor loving friends can hurt you,
    If all men count with you, but none too much;
If you can fill the unforgiving minute
    With sixty seconds' worth of distance run,
Yours is the Earth and everything that's in it,
    And—which is more—you'll be a Man, my son!

Or as I like to say, then you'll be a leader, my
good man (&/or good woman :-) So never settle,
never give up, & keep elevating beyond!

— Mark Minard

ACKNOWLEDGMENTS

It would take another book to thank all the people I need to! I want to say a special thank you to all the Mr & Mrs Awesome Faces out there, who God always brings into my life at the perfect season.

Sometimes they are challenging me to grow; other times they bring me encouragement, unity, or even just a great laugh!

I want to thank all the amazing families who have been so supportive of Dreamshine throughout the years. I'm so grateful to all of you.

To all our amazing individuals with developmental disabilities we are honored to serve at Dreamshine, you are my heroes! You remind me every day of my "why," you make the world a better place, and are the ones who have, indeed, changed my life. You are brave. You are beautiful, and you don't have disabilities; you have superpowers. Every time you smile, I see the beautiful light of God.

To all of *you*, who have supported my podcast over the years, my books, my content on social media, and each of you reading this book. I love you so much! I'm so blessed and honored to have the best humans on the planet supporting my work sharing your stories of how it has helped you become a better leader, husband, wife, mother, father, friend, and how you are killing it in your business. I'm so proud of you! You are the backbone of the economy, and when so many others run away from the "fire," you, the leaders, run into the fire, sacrificing yourself for the betterment of others. The world needs great leaders more than ever, so remember, You Don't Get To Give Up!

To my beautiful wife Iyeba, my five children, BK, Mo, Neveah, Harjanah, and little Gil—I love you all more than you can possibly imagine.

To my parents, Vicki & Gil Minard, and my sister, Amy Minard, I love you all so much.

To every editor, every team member who has been a part of this three-year adventure in creating this book, thank you. We have worked our butts off, and I never could have done it without all of you!

To the greatest serving leader ever, Jesus Christ, all the glory goes to you. You are where my "why" starts, and ends. You are my rock. Thank you for never giving up on me and for loving me unconditionally.

ABOUT THE AUTHOR

Mark Minard went from jail at age 17 to building his own company at age 26 at the peak of the 2008 recession.

He is now the CEO & owner of Dreamshine, which has proudly served individuals with developmental disabilities for 13 years and counting.

Mark is also a worldwide speaker on leadership and personal development. *16 Reasons Why Your Business Sucks* is his second book. His first, *The Story of You*, shows readers how to transform adversity into adventure and take dreams to the next level.

Proud to be hitting more than four million downloads, Mark is the host of the world-famous *Elevating Beyond* Podcast, ranked in the iTunes top 100.

Mark is a husband and father of five (so please don't come to him with the excuse that you don't have enough time to be awesome.) Mark's just an ordinary dude, with an extraordinary faith, believing all things are possible.

CPSIA information can be obtained
at www.ICGtesting.com
Printed in the USA
LVHW091035080920
664817LV00039BA/489

9 781734 742909